BUILDING A KINGDOM BUSINESS: A VIEW FROM THE TRENCHES

HOW YOU CAN CREATE A BUSINESS WITH SIGNIFICANCE AND IMPACT FOR GOD

Scott A. McClymonds

Building a Kingdom Business: A View From the Trenches
How You Can Create A Business With Significance
And Impact For God
by Scott A. McClymonds

Printed in the United States of America

ISBN 9781615790968

www.xulonpress.com

Do you view your business or job as merely a means to earn a living, or as a force to impact the world for Jesus Christ? Do you have a burning passion for doing a great work for the Lord, but have not yet figured out how to accomplish it due to time or financial constraints? Do you feel you need to do more with your work life than just punch a clock? Are you looking for ways to better motivate your employees? Would you like to better balance your life among business, family, and church? Do you want to become a better leader? All these questions will be addressed for you in the following pages.

Here is what some business leaders just like you have to say about what you are about to embark upon:

"This book provides important teaching by following a scriptural model and real example of how one Christian took a calling and passion to serve the Lord in business and thoughtfully and honestly leads us through the real challenges of putting this into play through risk taking and overcoming the many challenges that come against a kingdom business venture. This book provides a framework for all who seek to take back a piece of this world, all who have felt a similar call, with words of faith and encouragement that we can humbly impact our culture today and His kingdom for eternity when we submit all to His kingdom call."
—James M. Barthel, President and CEO, MT2, LLC—
Metals Treatment Technologies

"Scott illuminates powerful principles from Nehemiah into a template for successful business applications. I have observed him implement these principles into his own business from the beginning with success over multiple obstacles."
—Jim Beckman, MD, Physician and Business Owner

ACKNOWLEDGEMENTS

Thank you, Cindy, my love and support.

Thanks, Mom and Dad, and Walt and Winnie.
We're sunk without you guys.

TABLE OF CONTENTS

But you will receive power when the Holy Spirit has come upon you, and you will be my witnesses in Jerusalem and in all Judea and Samaria, and to the end of the earth.

Acts 1:8

The kingdom of heaven is like a grain of mustard seed that a man took and sowed in his field. It is the smallest of all seeds, but when it has grown it is larger than all the garden plants and becomes a tree, so that the birds of the air come and make nests in its branches.

Matthew 13:31-32

I will put enmity between you and the woman, and between your offspring and her offspring; he shall bruise your head, and you shall bruise his heel.

Genesis 3:15

For we are his workmanship, created in Christ Jesus for good works, which God prepared beforehand, that we should walk in them.

Ephesians 2:10

And I heard the voice of the Lord saying, "Whom shall I send, and who will go for us?" Then I said, "Here am I! Send me."

Isaiah 6:8

But someone will say, "You have faith and I have works." Show me your faith apart from your works, and I will show you my faith by my works.

James 2:18

Only let your manner of life be worthy of the gospel of Christ, so that whether I come and see you or am absent, I may hear of you that you are standing firm in one spirit, with one mind striving side by side for the faith of the gospel.

Philippians 1:27

Count it all joy, my brothers, when you meet trials of various kinds, for you know that the testing of your faith produces steadfastness. And let steadfastness have its full effect, that you may be perfect and complete, lacking in nothing.

James 1:2-4

But if you bite and devour one another, watch out that you are not consumed by one another.

Galatians 5:15

You will be hated by all for my name's sake. But the one who endures to the end will be saved.

Matthew 10:22

Moses' father-in-law said to him, "What you are doing is not good. You and the people with you will certainly wear yourselves out, for the thing is too heavy for you. You are not able to do it alone.

Exodus 18:17-18

Are not two sparrows sold for a penny? And not one of them will fall to the ground apart from your Father. But even the hairs of your head are all numbered. Fear not, therefore; you are of more value than many sparrows.

Matthew 10:29-31

Each one's work will become manifest, for the Day will disclose it, because it will be revealed by fire, and the fire will test what sort of work each one has done. If the work that anyone has built on the foundation survives, he will receive a reward.

1 Corinthians 3:13-14

You did not choose me, but I chose you and appointed you that you should go and bear fruit and that your fruit should abide, so that whatever you ask the Father in my name, he may give it to you.

John 15:16

If we say we have no sin, we deceive ourselves, and the truth is not in us. If we confess our sins, he is faithful and just to forgive us our sins and to cleanse us from all unrighteousness. If we say we have not sinned, we make him a liar, and his word is not in us.

1 John 1:8-10

CHAPTER 15.....169
The People Make a Covenant With God:
Nehemiah Chapter 10

But be doers of the word, and not hearers only, deceiving yourselves.

James 1:22

CHAPTER 16.....185
The Kingdom People Move Into the New City:
Nehemiah Chapter 11

You are the light of the world. A city set on a hill cannot be hidden.

Matthew 5:14

CHAPTER 17.....191
The Kingdom People Celebrate God's Goodness:
Nehemiah Chapter 12

And I heard every creature in heaven and on earth and under the earth and in the sea, and all that is in them, saying, "To him who sits on the throne and to the Lamb be blessing and honor and glory and might forever and ever!"

Revelation 5:13

CHAPTER 18.....197
The Kingdom People Return to Their Old Ways:
Nehemiah Chapter 13

And they came to Jerusalem. And he entered the temple and began to drive out those who sold and those who bought in the temple, and he overturned the tables of the money-changers and the seats of those who sold pigeons.

Mark 11:15

CHAPTER 19.....205
Your Response to God's Word

Now those who were scattered went about preaching the word.

Acts 8:4

INTRODUCTION

But you will receive power when the Holy Spirit has come upon you, and you will be my witnesses in Jerusalem and in all Judea and Samaria, and to the end of the earth.

Acts 1:8

Thank you for choosing this book. Through it, I hope to inspire you to do great things for Christ through your business, your influence, and your skills. In order to do this, we are going to explore the actions of an amazing Old Testament man named Nehemiah. His love for God and His people motivated him to do the "impossible" for God's kingdom, and I am hopeful that our examination of him will convince you that God can use you to have a similar or even greater impact. We will look at each chapter of Nehemiah from a business standpoint, and it will become a model for us to develop a kingdom business that serves Christ's church.

Yes, that's what I said. Our businesses serve the church—not necessarily the physical location defined by the four walls of the places we worship on Sundays; rather, the church universal, the body of believers throughout the world. In Ephesians, we are told that God the Father has placed all things under the authority of Jesus Christ, the Head of the church. All of history is leading up to the new heavens and the new earth, when the church will reign with Christ as the Head. Everything will be transformed back to its originally intended, sinless state, and that includes business.

Before we reach that point, the realm of business still falls under Christ's authority, and our job as entrepreneurs and business leaders is to reclaim business for Christ in a way that brings glory to Him and builds His church, otherwise known as the kingdom of God. Like all things in life, business is corrupted by sin through the fall, but since Christ saved us, He is calling us through His power to do our best to conform everything to its original, sinless condition, including business. Far from arguing we will have sinless business this side of heaven, I am stating that He calls us to be radically different from the world, and to do business according to His principles.

One of the ways we can reclaim business for Christ and build His kingdom is to do what is said in Romans 12, which is to be transformed by the renewing of our minds and not be conformed to the ways of the world. This means we search the Scriptures and let them guide our business practices instead of letting them be shaped by the world. It means we question everything we do to understand whether or not it conforms to Scripture.

I think you will enjoy seeing how Nehemiah integrated this line of thinking into his vision and actions to help build God's kingdom. You will see he was a "regular guy" like the rest of us, but God used him to do extraordinary things because he was willing to take risks, be faithful, and be used.

As I write this in 2009, it is no secret that the world is struggling economically. Many are looking to governments and politicians to provide the answers to complex social and economic issues. As I have stated, this book takes a different perspective, one that acknowledges that, despite the difficult times we face, God is still God, and His promises are the same in good times and bad ones. His promises are timeless, and our God is always faithful to fulfill them. So we look to Him for direction and mercy instead of to governments and politicians because we recognize His sovereign and mighty power over all things.

This book also recognizes that God's mighty power working through the efforts of passionate and motivated individuals and families can accomplish unimaginably good things for His kingdom. One of the many timeless characteristics of God is that He uses His people to bring about His purposes, and that includes entrepreneurs and business leaders like you. This book is directed toward Christian entrepreneurs and business leaders who want to be used mightily by God to build His kingdom and who want to stand for Him in these perilous times. In Philippians chapter 2, the apostle Paul tells us to shine as lights in the world, and this book is directed toward those of you who are committed to shining as lights through your businesses.

The world needs deeply committed, passionate, Christian business people right now. It needs leadership from people like you and me who are resolute not only about conducting our business in a way that glorifies God, but who are also intent upon having God use their business as a tool to bring Christ to the nations. Let's face it, business is powerful, and entrepreneurship is one of the most powerful activities in business. We use our businesses to influence customers, employees, and vendors, but our businesses also can impact generations of people. That's what this book is about, using your business to impact generations of people for the gospel of Jesus Christ. Without a doubt, Christians who are gifted in business can be used mightily by God in building His kingdom and can have a profound impact on society for years to come.

In short, this book is a call to radical action. Not the kind that is anti-government or that results in protests or civil disobedience. Rather, this book calls on Christian entrepreneurs and business leaders to pray and ask God to use them in making a significant and lasting impact for His kingdom at a time when the world is at a crossroads. Now is the time to pray, to call on God's mighty power, and to act in the name of Jesus to build kingdom businesses and teach and model kingdom-building business principles to the next generation of young Christians. You are about to read about a man who did this very thing many years ago and forever changed the world. I invite you to prayerfully join him and learn his model for kingdom building, which has impacted generations of Christians, even today.

<u>What to Expect From This Book</u>

Our analysis of Nehemiah will serve as a model for starting and operating a kingdom-based business, and for dealing with the challenges you will face as the entrepreneur behind such a business. It will not contain every verse or principle of Scripture applicable to a kingdom business, but it will show you how to apply Scripture, prayer, and faith, especially in difficult situations. It will show you how to do business differently from the world and give you confidence in God's faithfulness to honor your efforts.

Throughout these pages, our primary focus will be to explore how this incredibly amazing and devout man built the equivalent of a kingdom business, which positively influenced many generations of people. In fact, it could easily be argued that what he did impacts all of Christianity today. One man, operating with faith, courage, passion, and skill, changed an entire society because he was willing to answer God's call. As a result of Nehemiah's willingness, God unleashed His incredible power to rebuild a society and pave the way for Jesus Christ to come. I argue that God is no less at work through you than He was through Nehemiah. He is calling you, someone who as a business leader is gifted very similarly to Nehemiah. He can and will do great things through you and your business if you listen to His call and respond to it in faith.

While the book of Nehemiah gives us a great example that we can use to help us build our kingdom businesses, it is not to say that we must follow it precisely. Rather, he gives us principles that a godly entrepreneur can use to build a solid business that brings glory to God and significantly influences the world for Christ.

The pattern we will use in attempting to understand and follow Nehemiah's example is to look at the Scripture, analyze Nehemiah's actions in light of business, and then draw some applications for you to use. Then we will have sections titled "Views From the Trenches," where we will examine my family's business, Busy Bees Christian PreSchool, Inc. By looking at Busy Bees, you will see we have used the principles in Nehemiah to guide our business. We will try to be as honest as possible with you about the things we did right, as well as those we did wrong. From that I trust that you will then be able to apply them to your own business.

We use the example of Busy Bees because I want you to see that using the book of Nehemiah as a blueprint for building a kingdom business is not a matter of mere philosophy. It comes as a result of living this book during the last four or five years as my wife, Cindy, and I have planned and opened a Christian preschool. Understanding the principles lived out by Nehemiah literally kept our business open during its worst times and gave us the faith to keep going.

By writing this, I hope to inspire you in the same way, not by giving you a pep talk or making you feel good, but by helping you understand the book of Nehemiah as it applies to your business, and by using real examples from our own business to help you see how vital Nehemiah is even today. It remains vital, of course, because it is God's timeless Word. From experience, I know that applying the book of Nehemiah can help you develop a stronger vision and purpose for your business. It is my prayer that by learning to apply the book of Nehemiah to your business, you will realize how important your business is to God's kingdom and gain an understanding of the difference between a Christian business and a kingdom business.

If you are an existing or prospective Christian entrepreneur or a leader in someone else's company, this book is meant to challenge you to pray and focus on how God can use you and your business to help expand His kingdom. This book is also meant to inspire you to prayerfully and wisely take risks for the kingdom through your business using the template God gives us in Nehemiah. Nehemiah weaves together prayer, skill, faith, courage, and vision. By following the model he has laid out for us, you can ask the Lord to help you apply the same key skills and character traits in your business.

At the end of this book, my aspiration is that you will be able to develop a far-reaching vision for how your business can impact God's kingdom, not just through the goods and services you provide your customers, or the kind way in which you treat your employees and customers, but also as a means to generate capital to fund missionaries, build new churches and pay off the debt on existing ones, help the poor, and teach younger generations how to build businesses that glorify God.

From this book you will see how Nehemiah teaches us to build and lead a team, prepare for adversity, and have a greater sense of how to balance work, family, and church. My prayer is that you will be so invigorated by Nehemiah that you will share his story with your friends, partners, and family.

This book is not a book on sales, marketing, finance, strategic planning, or operations. There are many great books available on those topics, and throughout the book, I will mention several authors who have influenced me. I don't propose to waste your time here by recycling someone else's business material. However, you will see real life examples of all of those topics both throughout Nehemiah as well as from Busy Bees Christian PreSchool. This book gives you the biblical foundation you will need to bring all of those necessary elements together in a kingdom-oriented, Christ-centered business.

Author's Background

A missionary friend of mine, Paul Huey of Wycliffe Bible Translators, read the first rough draft of this book and suggested I include a section to give you a little insight into my background. Taking Paul's advice, I have included this section so you can understand the background of the person whose work you are reading. You will find that my family and I are just normal people. But God has a long history of using normal people, so as you read this part, I hope you will think about your own background and how God can use it. Most people have more skill and wisdom than they give themselves credit for, so I hope this will stimulate your thinking. Here goes.

My wife, Cindy, and I have been married for almost sixteen years, and both of us grew up in Christian homes. God, church, family, friends, our country, and our businesses are our top priorities. We are unashamed to claim Jesus Christ as our Lord and Savior. He gives the ultimate meaning and motivation in our lives.

Serving in our church is an integral part of our lives, as are our children, Andrew and Emilia. Cindy is actively involved in children's ministries and home schools our children. I serve as an elder and have had many opportunities to teach the Bible to people of all ages. We believe in a strong Christian worldview, meaning all aspects of life fall under God's dominion, not just church. That's the message of the Bible, and we try our best to live that way, albeit imperfectly.

In addition to church and family, I have a full-time job, and we own two businesses, Busy Bees Christian PreSchool, Inc., and McClymonds Enterprises, LLC, a real estate investment company. We try to incorporate a Christian worldview into our businesses, and since this is a business book that illustrates how to build a kingdom-based business, I would like to give you a brief overview of my business background so you can have confidence that I am an experienced practitioner as opposed to a mere philosopher.

First, I am an unashamed and unabashed capitalist. I love business, love free enterprise, and love creating products and services for people to buy and enjoy. I believe in making a profit, and enjoy the challenge of managing and leading a business in such a way that it actually makes money. For those of you who own your own businesses, you know how much skill and tenacity is required to be profitable.

I see no dichotomy between being a Christian and making a profit, nor will I apologize to anyone for making one. In fact, I believe the Bible provides many principles for us to apply so that we can make a profit. The Bible gives us examples of how to make a profit by being productive with our labor, and it also gives us many admonitions to not abuse our workers or use our profits to lavish luxuries upon ourselves.

Regarding my specific experience, I have worked in the banking industry in the field of database marketing for about twenty years. The last eleven have been spent managing a database marketing unit for a large regional bank in Arkansas, where I am still employed. Prior to that, I worked for large banks in similar, but lower-level, capacities.

While working full time for a bank in Columbus, Ohio, I received a master's degree in business administration from the Ohio State University in the evenings. Go Bucks. I have always excelled as a student and employee in corporate America, but never had any training as an entrepreneur. I knew a lot about business, but in all my training never really seriously considered being a business owner. I did not come from an entrepreneurial family. Rather, we all went to college and went to work for corporations. All my education as an entrepreneur came from investing literally thousands of hours and dollars in self-study books and courses, as well as from hands-on experience.

In 1997, at the age of thirty-five, I was laid off from my job at a bank in Virginia. The company had been acquired, and almost

40 percent of the work force was let go. At the time, Cindy and I lived close to our families and attended a church we loved. Instead of being able to continue that lifestyle, God decided to bring us to Arkansas.

We were happy to move to Arkansas and were thankful to God for providing a job. We realized that just like He did with Abraham, God still moves His people around. Nevertheless, I also decided that I wanted to start a business on the side in order to produce income in the event of another layoff. When both sets of our parents eventually moved to Arkansas, our focus on this became even more intent because we did not want to have to move again and leave our parents behind.

The initial business we started was building, buying, and renting houses. After about eight years, we have a nice portfolio of single-family rental homes we own and manage. That business was a good first step out of the corporate "ivory tower" because it provided us with flesh-and-blood customers and enhanced our sales and negotiating skills. It got us started thinking as business owners and investors instead of as employees, a major breakthrough since there is an enormous difference in the mind-sets of each.

This business remains a good one, but rental houses do not produce much cash flow until they are paid off. They are still good investments, but since our goals were to pay them off sooner than later in order to help replace my bank income, if necessary, we decided to try to pay our houses off faster by starting a business that generated more cash flow.

The Start of Busy Bees Christian PreSchool, Inc.

In the fall of 2004, Cindy and I attended a world missions conference at our church, which challenged us to find a way to reach our community for the gospel. We saw missionaries reaching people for Christ in various parts of the world and felt called to follow their lead by doing something to take the gospel to our hometown in Arkansas.

On the advice of a friend, and after much research and prayer, we decided to start a Christian preschool. Our research indicated that a Christian preschool would enable us to achieve our goals of reaching our community for Christ, impacting our culture generationally through children, and creating cash flow that would support us whether or not we had traditional jobs. In addition, it seemed that a preschool would not require Cindy or me to be on site regularly, which is important since I still have my full-time bank job and Cindy has her hands full homeschooling Andrew and Emilia.

With these things in mind, we began Busy Bees Christian PreSchool, Inc., in 2006, naively thinking we would soon be full, profitable, and winning souls for the Lord. Well, things didn't exactly work out the way we expected.

Despite my experience in business, my hours of study, my belief and faith in God, and the very detailed preparation that went into Busy Bees, I have to tell you we were not prepared for the rigors and stress of owning a business that is open every day. At times, the stress has been unimaginable, unlike anything I have ever experienced in corporate America or even real estate.

Nevertheless, God has faithfully seen us through even the darkest of times, largely by encouraging us through the book of Nehemiah as well as other parts of Scripture. While we have had plenty of struggles, we also have been very encouraged by the fact that we have impacted several hundred children, parents, and employees for the gospel, and have had many wonderful compliments and accolades from parents and the community we serve.

Although there are still large challenges at Busy Bees, things are much better now than they were several years ago. We have had tremendous financial improvements each year, and have a legitimate shot at making a profit in 2009. Survival throughout the first two years was a miracle, though, and Cindy and I could only have gotten through it by God's strength and help, along with the advice and prayers of our parents and fellow church members.

During the first year of operation, I read through the Old Testament historical books from Joshua to Nehemiah. These were books of the Bible I wasn't very familiar with, and I wanted to understand them better. Fortunately, I had the opportunity to teach both the books of Joshua and Nehemiah in Sunday school and in a small group. While my study of these books was not motivated by our involvement with Busy Bees, they ended up having a profound influence on the business.

Without a doubt, these two books were the scriptural encouragement we needed to keep the school open and get through all the turmoil and stress of the first couple of years. Both of these Old Testament men were inspirational heroes in their own ways. Joshua used his faithfulness and tenacity to lead the Israelites in conquering many nations throughout his lifetime. Nehemiah shows us his sense of calling, passion for God's people, and willingness to do big picture kingdom work.

Nehemiah was especially striking to me, as I felt Cindy and I were living the book of Nehemiah every day with our business. While I constantly studied many great business writers and thinkers, such as Dan Kennedy, Michael Gerber, Nido Qubein, and Dave Ramsey, more than anyone else, I frequently found myself reflecting on Nehemiah and trying to follow his example.

Since I have taught the book of Nehemiah now two times and have lived it for several years, I feel God has been calling me to share my insights and experiences with this marvelous book, and show you how it can be used as a template for you to run a Christian business that can have a far-reaching impact for God's kingdom. I have been encouraged by the writings of many entrepreneurs and hope to particularly encourage those of you who are just starting out, when you are most vulnerable.

I am sharing it with you now while we are in the third year of our business so that I can describe to you as clearly as possible the challenges and rewards we have experienced in starting a kingdom-based business. I will not sugarcoat things for you by promising you success simply by following Nehemiah's "formula." That would be misleading and would not be a good service to you. Instead, I want to help you follow Nehemiah's pattern through fervent prayer, courage, and a love for God and His people. Just as Nehemiah had no guarantee of success, neither do you or I. Nevertheless, we press on just like he did until the Lord calls us to stop. Cindy and I are neither famous nor extraordinarily successful. Rather, we are ordinary Christians trying to do something extraordinary for God's kingdom. We hope our story woven into the template of Nehemiah will inspire you to make a difference for God's kingdom through your business.

By using our story to provide a modern-day account of the Scripture, I hope to encourage you if you are struggling in your own business, looking for the next level in your business, or just contemplating starting a business.

Let's get started.

Chapter 1

The Case for a Kingdom Business

The kingdom of heaven is like a grain of mustard seed that a man took and sowed in his field. It is the smallest of all seeds, but when it has grown it is larger than all the garden plants and becomes a tree, so that the birds of the air come and make nests in its branches.

Matthew 13:31-32

All of human history is converging to a point where there will be a new heaven and a new earth, where the church of Christ will rule over the nations, with Jesus Christ as its Head. In Revelation chapter 21, we are given a stunning account of how all things will be made new by Christ and the church will be "prepared as a bride adorned for her husband." The new Jerusalem, otherwise known as the church, is referred to as "the Bride, the wife of the Lamb." This culmination of Christ's redemptive work will result in our worshiping and glorifying Him forever. At this point, I am certain that what is written in Philippians 2:10-11 will be true, "that at the name of Jesus every knee should bow, in heaven and on earth and under the earth, and every tongue confess that Jesus Christ is Lord, to the glory of God the Father."

What does the fact that the church will reign with Christ at the Head have to do with your business? These Scriptures let us know that Jesus Christ is primarily concerned with the redemption and perfection of His bride, the church, in order that God's people might enjoy the perfect fellowship for which they were created. From a business standpoint, it tells us to prioritize our efforts according to those of our Head, Christ. If Christ is focused on building and perfecting the church, so should we through our businesses.

I invite you to consider several passages in Ephesians to further strengthen these points in your mind. First, Ephesians 1:22-23 tells us, "And he put all things under his feet and gave him as head over all things to the church, which is his body, the fullness of him who fills all in all." By saying all things are under His feet, the apostle Paul means every aspect of human endeavor falls under the authority of Jesus Christ. Everything, business included, is under His authority. Obviously, now it is imperfect, but it will be perfected in the new heaven and earth. In saying "to the church," Paul means the universal body of believers, all Christians. All our endeavors are to be under the authority of Christ in order to bring glory to Him and His bride, the church. The church is referred to as "the fullness of him who fills all in all." I believe that refers to the new Jerusalem and shows us that the perfected church is the focal point of His work.

In Ephesians 2:10, we are told that the purpose of our salvation is to do the works that God prepared beforehand for us, and in Ephesians 3:20-21, Scripture tells of God's amazing power at work within us in order to bring glory to Christ and His church. Clearly, God brings about this perfecting of the church through the individual and collective efforts of individuals, families, and all His chosen people throughout the entire world.

Taking this a step further, Romans 12:1 tells us that as a result of the great mercy provided to us by Christ, we should present our bodies as living sacrifices, "holy and acceptable to God." In the verses immediately after this, Paul directs us to use our gifts for the benefit of the church. For the business owner and leader, that means we are to strive for excellence in our businesses in ways that honor Christ and build His church.

The essence of all these Scriptures is to lead us to the conclusion that the ultimate purpose of our lives and businesses is to bring glory to Christ by building His church. When we refer to His church, it is the same as referring to His kingdom. Since Christ goes to the greatest efforts imaginable to build His church, any business that seeks to glorify Him also should seek to aggressively, assertively focus its efforts on building God's kingdom.

Because of this, I believe there is a difference between a Christian business and a kingdom business. They are similar in that their owners are Christian and do their best to uphold Christian principles in their businesses. Both seek to honor Jesus by treating their customers and employees with respect, selling high-quality goods and services, and providing outstanding customer service. These are traits every Christian should strive for in his business, and I believe God will honor him for it. The distinguishing characteristic between a Christian and a kingdom business is the vision of each type of business.

The vision of a Christian business is to operate profitably and in a way that shows its customers the love of Christ by the way it treats its customers and employees. It may be a good member of civic organizations. There is much good in every way in this type of business. However, its vision is often limited to the here and now. Often the entrepreneur sees it as no more than a job, a means to earn a living. There is nothing wrong with this, but its limited vision tends to underutilize the assets of the business in terms of how they can be used for God's kingdom.

In contrast, kingdom businesses operate with a larger vision in mind. The vision of a kingdom business goes far beyond the products or services the business sells. In fact, the vision may often be generational; that is, going beyond the lifetime of the owner. The mind of the kingdom-building entrepreneur considers his or her business not only as an income source, but also as a resource to be used by God for the expansion of His kingdom. Such an entrepreneur knows he must build a strong and profitable business to support the needs of his family. Beyond that, however, he is concerned about making his company more profitable and successful, not to live an opulent lifestyle, but to have an increasingly large impact on the growth of God's kingdom. His passion is far beyond mere income generation and survival. His drive is to use whatever business skills and opportunities God has given him to have a potentially massive impact for God's kingdom by creating capital and other resources to glorify Christ and His church.

A kingdom entrepreneur, with a vision of generating capital for God's kingdom, realizes that a successful kingdom business has the capacity to provide many more resources for God's kingdom than any one individual family. From a financial perspective, he realizes the capital his business produces can build new hospitals, plant new churches, help existing churches become debt-free, fund missionary movements, create Christian schools and colleges, and provide training and education to the poor.

Perhaps even more important than the creation of financial capital, a kingdom entrepreneur realizes the human capital he can develop can last for generations. By human capital, he means the development of a solid employee base that understands his vision and passionately embraces it and moves it forward. Such an entrepreneur knows he has to have a strong team motivated by his goals and moving in the same direction toward his vision. Without this creation of human capital, the financial capital created by the kingdom entrepreneur may run out if no one is left to perpetuate the company after the entrepreneur is gone. With this in mind, the kingdom entrepreneur knows he must develop his employees both from a business and spiritual standpoint if he wants his vision to continue.

A kingdom entrepreneur understands that he must continually hone and increase his business skills in order to achieve the level of business success required to attain his kingdom goals. This type of entrepreneur realizes God will not supernaturally suspend the time-tested and well-known rules of best practice businesses simply because he is Christian, nor will He automatically bring great customers and employees to him. Instead, he knows he must become excellent at what he does and makes a lifelong commitment to improve his skills by studying marketing, sales, finance, operations, and personnel development. He is committed to excellence in customer service, quality in his products and services, and profitability in his business because he knows he must achieve those ideals in order to maximize his impact on the kingdom. Moreover, the kingdom entrepreneur is not naive enough to believe that success will come quickly or easily. He knows he will have to struggle, fight, and go through many disappointments and difficult trials before accomplishing his goals.

A kingdom entrepreneur is characterized by a love of God and knowledge of Scripture, an impassioned vision for building God's kingdom, a humble and repentant heart, the knowledge that great things can only be achieved through God's power, and a commitment to both prayer and well-thought-out action.

As we study Nehemiah, we will see all of these characteristics at work, as well as the following ones:

- A well-planned vision, organizational structure, and funding
- An organized approach to work that maximizes and rewards the accomplishments of its workers
- The strength to overcome internal and external adversity
- A faith that trusts God to see the mission through
- Repentance and forgiveness among the team members for sins committed
- Detailed attention to data processing and record maintenance
- A strong commitment to and definition of core values
- A commitment to family
- Faithful serving and use of gifts in churches
- Perseverance—not giving up
- A willingness to discipline, or terminate people who violate the business principles and potentially derail the vision of the business
- Fairness and impartiality
- Generosity—being mindful of the poor, needy, and oppressed

The full impact of kingdom entrepreneurs' efforts might not be fulfilled for generations. They may not see the full fruit of their efforts. We will see that despite the success Nehemiah had in leading Israel in building the wall around Jerusalem (the product), it was very difficult to maintain a strong team after their initial success.

The people went back to their natural sinful inclinations, and it took a fierce rekindling of Nehemiah's impassioned vision to keep the people together. Kingdom entrepreneurs know their leadership is required to keep the fires of their organizations lit, and that's why the study of this Old Testament leader is so critical.

As we embark upon our examination of kingdom business building by studying Nehemiah, we will do so first by examining a broader set of Scriptures with the goal of understanding God's eternal plan as well as the way God uses His chosen people to bring about His purposes. Nehemiah had a thorough understanding of Scripture, and he used it to fuel his passion and vision. If we are to follow the example of Nehemiah, we need to commit to acquiring his level of understanding and application of God's Word. The next two chapters are designed to provide a foundation for gaining that level of understanding, but they are by no means a substitute for a lifelong commitment to studying God's Word.

View From the Trenches

From my perspective, building a kingdom business requires an unusually high level of energy and drive. In my household, it entails reading and studying, applying and testing, coaching and directing, and reassessing and continuing the innovation cycle. The differentiator between a traditional entrepreneur and a kingdom entrepreneur is the spiritual vigilance that must be applied to the kingdom business. Without Cindy's and my vigilance in this area, our business would become secularized because our employees would drift in that direction even though they are Christians. We try to keep in mind that God laid this venture on *our* hearts; therefore, we are the keepers of it. If we do not feed and nurture that vision, carefully cultivating it within our business, Busy Bees will become just like any other preschool, and our reason for existence will have died. Even though it is extremely difficult at times, we try to stay focused on this aspect of the business. Admittedly, we have failed from time to time, but praying to God for strength and mercy continually rescues and revives us, and He picks us up so we can keep going. Of course, keeping up the spiritual intensity requires making sure we are being fed and nurtured within our church, through individual study, weekly fellowship with other believers, and ministering in the church.

Chapter 2

God's Eternal Plan and Your Business

I will put enmity between you and the woman, and between your offspring and her offspring; he shall bruise your head, and you shall bruise his heel.

Genesis 3:15

It is common knowledge in business that failing to plan is planning to fail. I suspect that you, like me, have not always planned things out as well as you would have liked. Maybe you didn't think through the various steps of your plan, or perhaps you neglected to properly envision or assess the potential consequences of your plans. Maybe you neglected to plan altogether.

Throughout this book, you will see the value of planning and adapting your strategies, taking special note of Nehemiah, observing the ups and downs of Busy Bees, and making application to your business. Before proceeding in that direction, however, we must first examine the greatest plan of all—God's eternal plan of salvation through Jesus Christ.

What does God's eternal plan of salvation have to do with your business? Everything. God is the God of history. He always has been, and always will be, the Author of history. That's what His plan is all about. He is sovereign and omnipotent. That means He is over everything, and there is no chance that what He plans will not come to pass.

The Bible clearly demonstrates that God takes a very active role in human history. Since your business is part of human history, it is only logical to assert that your business is part of God's sovereign and eternal plan. Maybe you never thought of your business this way. Perhaps you think your business is too small or trivial to be on God's "radar screen." Not so, fellow business leader. If we believe in God's sovereignty over history, then we must believe He is sovereign over *everything* within history. If anything was outside His sovereignty, He would not be sovereign. Since your business is part of history, it is only logical to conclude He is also sovereign over your business.

What does this mean for you? It means your business has always been part of God's eternal plan. It is not an accident you are where you are in your business. It's no accident that it exists. You are where you are in your business by God's perfect design. It is within God's perfect plan for you to have your business and to use it as a means to glorify Him and expand His kingdom. That is meant to give you great comfort and confidence as you proceed in building your business. He is sovereignly guiding you and your business according to His purpose, and that should be very encouraging. It also should direct you to realize there is no difference between your spiritual and work life. Every aspect of your life is under the umbrella of God's sovereignty, and should be treated as such.

While this is far from a book on theology, there are certain concepts we must understand in order to have a strong biblical foundation for building a kingdom-based business. Let's start by examining God's plan of redemption through Jesus Christ.

The Bible tells us that before the foundation of the world, God had a plan to redeem His chosen people through His Son, Jesus Christ. John 1: 1-4 says, "In the beginning was the Word, and the Word was with God, and the Word was God. He was in the beginning with God. All things were made through him, and without him was not any thing made that was made. In him was life, and the life was the light of men." Of course, these verses refer to Jesus Christ, who was with God the Father, and who was God the Son, from all eternity.

Now, just think how crazy it would be if God the Father and His Son, Jesus, were watching humanity, their creation, go through history, and suddenly they realized, *Things aren't going quite the way we planned. These humans are totally messing things up. They're full of wickedness and corruption. We didn't count on this when we made them. What are we going to do? Quick, let's think of something to get this whole thing back on track. Hey, that sounds like a great plan, Jesus. You go to earth, live a perfect life, die on the cross, come back to life, return to heaven, and we can make things right. Let's do it."*

Obviously, that sounds absurd, and it is absurd. Do we really think that God is caught off guard by mankind, or that God has a plan He's diligently trying to work, but we keep throwing Him off base so that He must continually adapt to fulfill His plan of redemption? It is complete foolishness to think such a thing.

On the contrary, if we believe the Bible proclaims God's sovereignty, then we realize He is all-powerful and almighty. Nothing can stop His plan to bring His chosen people into His kingdom, and nothing can stop His plan to bring glory and honor to His Son, Jesus Christ, the King of Kings.

Looking at some actual Bible verses will help us solidify our scriptural understanding of God's sovereign plan over history. We need look no further than the Old Testament to see evidence of how God said His plan would come about through Jesus Christ. The following verses are among the many that shed light on this:

1. Genesis 3:15 is the first promise of the Savior: "I will put enmity between you and the woman, and between your offspring and her offspring; he shall bruise your head, and you shall bruise his heel." This refers to Jesus' victory over Satan, even though for a time Jesus was persecuted and suffered.

2. Psalm 22 is known as a Messianic psalm, a psalm speaking of the Christ to come. In verses 16-18, it says, "They have

pierced my hands and feet—I can count all my bones—they stare and gloat over me; they divide my garments among them, and for my clothing they cast lots." These verses clearly reference the events of Jesus' crucifixion, which took place hundreds of years later.

3. Isaiah 9 is a famous passage read at Christmastime. We all know the words from verses 6 and 7: "For to us a child is born, to us a son is given; and the government shall be upon his shoulder, and his name shall be called Wonderful Counselor, Mighty God, Everlasting Father, Prince of Peace. Of the increase of his government and of peace there will be no end, on the throne of David and over his kingdom, to establish it and to uphold it with justice and with righteousness from this time forth and forevermore. The zeal of the LORD of hosts will do this."

4. Again in Isaiah 53, hundreds of years before Christ was born, the prophet said in verses 5 and 6, "But he was wounded for our transgressions; he was crushed for our iniquities; upon him was the chastisement that brought us peace, and with his stripes we are healed. All we like sheep have gone astray; we have turned—every one—to his own way; and the LORD has laid on him the iniquity of us all."

As if these Old Testament verses weren't enough to give ample evidence of God's plan from all eternity, we can turn to the following New Testament verses, which specifically reveal God's plan to save His people through Jesus Christ:

1. "But now the righteousness of God has been manifested apart from the law, although the Law and the Prophets bear witness to it—the righteousness of God through faith in Jesus Christ for all who believe" (Romans 3:21-22). These verses tell us that God's plan of salvation was being revealed to mankind through God's law given to Moses and through His messages to the Old Testament prophets.

2. "And we know that for those who love God all things work
    together for good, for those who are called according to his
    purpose. For those whom he foreknew he also predestined to
    be conformed to the image of his Son, in order that he might
    be the firstborn among many brothers. And those whom he
    predestined he also called, and those whom he called he
    also justified, and those whom he justified he also glorified"
    (Romans 8:28-30).

    > "Even as He chose us in Him before the foundation
    > of the world, that we should be holy and blameless
    > before him. In love he predestined us for adoption as
    > sons through Jesus Christ, according to the purpose
    > of his will" (Ephesians 1:4-5).

    In these two Scriptures, the apostle Paul tells us God had
    a plan and purpose in calling each of His, and that purpose
    was to be part of His adopted family.

3. ". . . making known to us the mystery of his will, according
    to his purpose, which he set forth in Christ as a plan for the
    fullness of time, to unite all things in him, things in heaven
    and things on earth" (Ephesians 1:9-10).

4. "In him we have obtained an inheritance, having been predes-
    tined according to the purpose of him who works all things
    according to the counsel of his will" (Ephesians 1:11).

    All of the above verses point to two things: the coming
    of Jesus Christ as King of Kings and Lord of Lords, and
    the salvation of God's chosen people. Clearly, God has an
    awesome plan for the building of His kingdom through Jesus
    Christ.

    How does this eternal plan of redemption through Jesus
    Christ come together with your building a kingdom busi-
    ness? All of human history begins and ends with Jesus Christ,
    according to God's plan. Since our businesses are part of

human history, that means the beginning and end of each of our businesses also should be Jesus Christ.

Of course, you cannot have a kingdom business unless you are first a child of the King. A Kingdom business starts with you, the entrepreneur, humbly bowing at the cross of Christ and asking Him to be your Lord and Savior. Without Christ at the center of your own life, you cannot have a Christ-centered business.

The next step is committing your business to being a kingdom business and operating it according to scriptural principles. That's what Nehemiah is going to help us explore starting in chapter 4.

One final point to consider before moving to chapter 3 is the fact that we have just shown that God is both a big picture and a detailed planner. If we are created in His image and are being conformed more and more to the image of His Son, Jesus, does it not make sense that we should also plan out our businesses as well as we can instead of rushing into them or operating them haphazardly? We'll examine this further in subsequent chapters as we go through the book of Nehemiah.

In chapter 3, we are going to continue laying the scriptural foundation for a kingdom business with a detailed look at what the Bible says about your part in carrying out God's plan through your business.

Chapter 3

How You and Your Business Fit Into God's Eternal Plan

For we are his workmanship, created in Christ Jesus for good works, which God prepared beforehand, that we should walk in them.

Ephesians 2:10

In the previous chapter, we considered God's eternal plan of redemption and His calling of His chosen people. We also defined God as sovereign and omnipotent over human history. Further, we concluded that your business is part of God's eternal plan since it, too, is part of human history. Accidents do not happen to God, so you are where you are by His design.

The Bible has much to say about how God uses specific individuals like you and me to help bring His plan into being. In fact, the entire Bible shows us example after example of how God's people are used mightily to build the kingdom. With this in mind, we are going to study several Scripture passages in this chapter that will show beyond a shadow of a doubt that God has a specific plan for you and your business.

From the following verses of Scripture, you will see that God does indeed have a plan for you in His kingdom. You are significant, and what you do matters a great deal for God's kingdom. In His great mercy and power, God weaves together the various personalities, gifts, and interests of his people throughout all generations to bring about His eternal plan. In other words, not only did God have His plan of redemption from all eternity; He also knew He would work His plan through weak, frail people like you and me. We are fortunate to be His instruments in carrying out His plan, and that means our work has great significance! See for yourself what the Scriptures say:

1. "For by grace you have been saved through faith. And this is not your own doing; it is the gift of God, not a result of works, so that no one may boast. For we are his workmanship, created in Christ Jesus for good works, which God prepared beforehand, that we should walk in them" (Ephesians 2:8-10).

   Do you realize that from all eternity, God had in mind the work He wanted you to do? This famous passage lets us know that we were saved from our sins through Jesus Christ for a reason—to do the vital work that God prepared for us based on the gifts, interests, and passions He has given us. He doesn't just have busy work for us to do. Instead, He has important work for us to do for His kingdom. We are here for a purpose—to do the work He has planned out specifically for each of us to do.

2. "Now to him who is able to do far more abundantly than all that we ask or think, according to the power at work within us, to him be glory in the church and in Christ Jesus throughout all generations, forever and ever. Amen" (Ephesians 3:20-21).

   Here we see God works through us and does extraordinary things through our ordinary lives, things we can't even imagine due to His unfathomable power. These verses hit me like a lightning bolt after I read the Old Testament passages, particularly in Joshua and Nehemiah.

   Time after time, we see God taking ordinary efforts of people like you and me and turning them into extraordinary results. Just like when Jesus fed the five thousand people with only a few loves and fishes, that is how He multiplies our small efforts and resources. It truly is amazing.

Think of the apostles and disciples in the early New Testament church. Even though there were relatively few of them, they were accused of turning the world upside down. How was this possible? It was due to God's power working in them to do "far more abundantly than all that we ask or think," according to His power working in us.

This is a key principle not to forget. All of us tend to get down from time to time, frequently discouraged by the progress we are making, sometimes wondering if our efforts are truly meaningful. We need not look any further than these verses to be reassured that it is God who is at work within us, and we can trust that His mighty power will expand even our most meager efforts for His kingdom.

These are just a few of the verses where God clearly shows that He carries out His plan for the expansion of His kingdom through common people like you and me. Salvation is through His Son, Jesus Christ, but He uses us to do the kingdom work of making disciples, leading others to Christ, and spreading the gospel throughout the world. It's a job we need to give serious thought and attention to as we consider how God has called and gifted each of us.

As business owners and leaders, we can use our business gifts to God's glory and make a profound difference for the kingdom. All of us want significance in our work. We all want to know that what we do matters, that our work somehow does good for other people. As Christians, we have God's promise that our work matters and that He will do incredible things through us. What a blessing! All we have to do is pray for God's leading, be willing to follow, and see where He takes us.

In the following chapter, we will begin our examination of how one man, Nehemiah, was used mightily by God to change the history of the Jewish nation, and perhaps Christianity as a whole. His faith, coupled with bold, prayerful actions, shows us that one person can have a massive impact on the world. We'll examine Nehemiah's faith, passion, struggles, leadership, wisdom, and commitment, and show how you can use his model to create kingdom businesses that God will use mightily to expand His kingdom.

View From the Trenches

In the previous two chapters, we have looked at a lot of Scripture in light of God's plan of redemption as well as His plan for you and your business. Some of you may feel like we've overdone it a little. Here's the method behind our madness: When times get tough, you need God's Word to fall back on, or you may give up, lose focus, go crazy, or otherwise snap under the stress. Look at how Jesus withstood the temptations of Satan. He constantly quoted God's Word. The same is true for the apostle Paul. How did he keep grounded despite being beaten, slandered, and imprisoned? His knowledge of the Word was impeccable.

We can verify from our own experience that the difficulties of our business have taken us almost to the brink of insanity. What saved us was having a strong foundation in God's Word. The longer we are in business, the more we know we must become more and more knowledgeable and skilled in applying His Word. It helps us stay focused on our main purpose, even though we frequently go through times of discouragement. We always seem to return to the positive and reassuring foundation of God's Word.

Not only does God's Word encourage and motivate us, but it specifically lets us examine the characteristics of God and some of the Bible's main characters. These, then, become our models. For example, in the previous chapter, we learned that God is a planner. Well, if it's okay for Him, that's probably something we should get good at, too, even though our natural inclination is toward disorganization and laxness. You're about to see someone else who was a good planner . . . Nehemiah.

Chapter 4

Listening for God's Inner Call:
Nehemiah Chapter 1

And I heard the voice of the Lord saying, "Whom shall I send, and who will go for us?" Then I said, "Here am I! Send me."

Isaiah 6:8

M any of us have had great ideas followed by rushes of excitement. Some new project we wanted to do, business we wanted to start, or website we wanted to design. We think if we can just put these ideas into action, our lives and those of our family members will be better, and many people will benefit from purchasing our new products and services. Unfortunately, many of our good ideas never come to fruition for a number of reasons.

In contrast, in this chapter, we begin to examine the call of Nehemiah. This is truly one of the most amazing passages in the entire Bible when we analyze it through the lens of each one of us answering God's call to do the work "which God prepared beforehand, that we should walk in." Nehemiah's response to God's inner call is just the opposite of our rejecting one of our own ideas, thinking it will never work. Nehemiah's actions proved he truly believed God's power would be at work in him to do "far more abundantly than all that we ask or think." He truly raised his hand and said, "Here am I! Send me." Let's take a look at the first chapter of Nehemiah, then consider it in terms of God's call to us as Christian business owners or leaders.

[1]The words of Nehemiah the son of Hacaliah.

Now it happened in the month of Chislev, in the twentieth year, as I was in Susa the capital, [2]that Hanani, one of my brothers, came with certain men from Judah. And I asked them concerning the Jews who escaped, who had survived the exile, and concerning Jerusalem. [3]And they said to me, "The remnant there in the province who had survived the exile is in great trouble and shame. The wall of Jerusalem is broken down, and its gates are destroyed by fire."

[4]As soon as I heard these words I sat down and wept and mourned for days, and I continued fasting and praying before the God of heaven. [5]And I said, "O LORD God of heaven, the great and awesome God who keeps covenant and steadfast love with those who love him and keep his commandments, [6]let your ear be attentive and your eyes open, to hear the prayer of your servant that I now pray before you day and night for the people of Israel your servants, confessing the sins of the people of Israel, which we have sinned against you. Even I and my father's house have sinned. [7]We have acted very corruptly against you and have not kept the commandments, the statutes, and the rules that you commanded your servant Moses. [8]Remember the word that you commanded your servant Moses, saying, 'If you are unfaithful, I will scatter you among the peoples, [9]but if you return to me and keep my commandments and do them, though your outcasts are in the uttermost parts of heaven, from there I will gather them and bring them to the place that I have chosen, to make my name dwell there.' [10]They are your servants and your people, whom you have redeemed by your great power and by your strong hand. [11]O Lord, let your ear be attentive to the prayer of your servant, and to the prayer of your servants who delight to fear your name, and give success to your servant today, and grant him mercy in the sight of this man."

Now I was cupbearer to the king.

To get some historical background, Nehemiah was an Israelite slave in exile as a result of the destruction of Jerusalem by the Babylonians described in 2 Chronicles chapter 36. God allowed Jerusalem to be destroyed as punishment for years of sin, idolatry, and a refusal to follow God. The Babylonians burned down God's temple, broke down the walls of Jerusalem, burned the city's palaces with fire, and destroyed all its precious possessions. Those inhabitants who were not killed were taken to Babylon, where they became servants.

Despite these terrible events, God worked through the hearts of Cyrus and other pagan kings to allow His people to return to Jerusalem within seventy years. In the book of Ezra, we read how God brought about incredible events to allow Ezra to lead a portion of the Israelites back to Israel in order to rebuild God's temple. However, some Israelites, Nehemiah being one of them, did not return to Jerusalem for whatever reason.

In Ezra chapter 7, we see that Ezra came to Jerusalem in the seventh year of the reign of King Artaxerxes, and in Nehemiah chapter 2, we see his actions taking place in the twentieth year of King Artaxerxes. So, assuming it is the same Artaxerxes in both cases, about thirteen years had passed between the time Ezra led the captives back to Jerusalem and the time Nehemiah first began to respond to God's call.

Since we are using the book of Nehemiah as a model to build your kingdom-based business, it is critically important to examine this beginning chapter of Nehemiah point by point. It has almost an overwhelming amount of substance to it, but it is so foundational that everything in it has to be in place within you if you are to build a true kingdom business. To help us understand it, we will break it into several sections.

The Concern: Verses 1-2

In verse 2, Nehemiah questioned his brother Hanani about the welfare of his countrymen living in Jerusalem, most of whom had been released from slavery in Babylon some time earlier. This question gives us a glimpse into Nehemiah's heart and lets us see his concern for God's people in Jerusalem. These were his native people, and he felt a close bond with them despite the distance that separated them. Any kingdom business starts with a love of God and His people, and a particular concern about a certain aspect of God's kingdom. For you to build a kingdom business, you will need to have a passionate interest in something, not just a particular aspect of business, but something that combines your business skills with the ability to address an area of need within God's kingdom. God's kingdom is big, and the needs among His people are numerous. You cannot address all the issues, nor does God want you to do that. He has gifted you uniquely, and in order for you to get going in the direction in which He has gifted you, you need to do some thinking and praying about where your interests lie, what problems really bother you, and what you really feel like doing something about. That was the starting point for Nehemiah.

The Need: Verse 3

The need of the Jewish exiles was clearly identified by Hanani and the other men. The people as well as their city had been devastated by the Babylonians between eighty and ninety years earlier, and they had not recovered. The Jews who had returned from Babylon were impoverished and defenseless. They lived among the pagan peoples of the land and were abused and mistreated by them. No doubt, they were the lowest rung of society. Furthermore, the walls and its gates were broken down, and the people had no protection. This lack of protection not only hurt them physically, but spiritually as well. They had no safe place to worship and no real way of uniting and encouraging each other as believers. In short, they were in danger of being wiped out as a people. Even if they somehow survived, without a way to protect and unite them, their culture and religion could very easily have been watered down by mixing in with the pagan peoples of the land.

It is here that we have to ask ourselves the following question as business leaders and entrepreneurs: Where do we see the people of God in extreme danger or need? Somewhere there is a broken and burned "wall" that we can address with our products and services, and we can begin by asking the Lord to open our eyes to see what "walls" are in need of repair.

Coming Boldly to the Throne of Grace Through Prayer: Verses 4-10

Hebrews 4:15-16 says the following about Jesus: "For we do not have a high priest who is unable to sympathize with our weaknesses, but one who in every respect has been tempted as we are, yet without sin. Let us then with confidence draw near to the throne of grace, that we may receive mercy and find grace to help in time of need."

This is exactly what Nehemiah did when he learned of the plight of God's people. He went to the throne of God's grace, boldly, humbly, contritely, and expectantly. Nehemiah 1:4 says he spent many days weeping, mourning, fasting, and praying. Clearly, his love of God and His people moved him to deep sorrow after he became aware of their dire circumstances. His first reaction was not to call for a hearing or some government intervention. This man of faith realized that God is more powerful than any invention of man, so Nehemiah went straight to the King of Kings. As we will see later, there was about a four-month time span between the time Nehemiah learned of the plight of the exiles and the time he first spoke to the king about it. Therefore, we know he prayed earnestly about this situation for at least four months.

What has God laid on your heart that will move you to pray earnestly, contritely, humbly, and expectantly? Is there something so huge, troubling, and seemingly impossible that you are concerned about? Take it diligently to Jesus in prayer. James 5:16 tells us the power of prayer by saying, "The prayer of a righteous person has great power as it is working." Nehemiah found out how much prayer can accomplish, and you and I can, too, if we follow Nehemiah's bold, humble, reverent, and expectant approach to God.

Examining Nehemiah's prayer, we see that he first acknowledged God's glory, majesty, and sovereignty, followed by His love and faithfulness. We can tell Nehemiah's prayer was an informed one because he knew exactly whom he was praying to. There was no question that Nehemiah was well-acquainted with the Bible and specifically what it had to say about God. Not only did he know the Bible; he also believed what it said. He counted it as completely truthful and was confident that it gave him a clear understanding that

God is who He says He is—almighty, great, awesome, and loving. Nehemiah's knowledge of and belief in the Scriptures led him to understand that God was infinitely more powerful than he was, and that a solution to so great a problem was dependent on God's mighty power and grace.

To build a kingdom business that addresses any significant issues, you and I must go to the Lord in informed prayer, knowing who He is, acknowledging our dependence on Him, and trusting that He has the power to solve the problem. We need to be students of His Word because it is the primary way He speaks to our hearts and gives us power, faith, and guidance. When you pray, do you praise God and thank Him for His goodness to you, or do you only offer up a wish list? Clearly, He wants us to express our needs to Him, but He also is honored as our King, Father, and Creator when we offer praise and thanksgiving to Him.

The second aspect of Nehemiah's prayer is asking God to be gracious toward him by listening to his prayers on behalf of his fellow countrymen. Note that his prayer was not for himself, but rather for God's people. It is instructive to see that Nehemiah thus far has not petitioned God for his own personal welfare. If you are to build a kingdom business, you must have an outward focus in your prayers for God's people. This requires having a love for God's people, which we mentioned previously. That was Nehemiah's driving motivation—love for God's people. It was also God the Father's motivation when He sent His only Son into the world. Are you motivated to pray earnestly and tirelessly for brothers and sisters in Christ?

The next part of Nehemiah's prayer is confession of sin, both for the nation of Israel as well as his own. He confesses the corruption of the Israelites and their overt disregard for God as well as His laws and ordinances. That we are sinners is not a newsflash to you or me. Despite our best efforts and intentions, we sin in every aspect of our lives, including our businesses. Sometimes we sin out of ignorance, and sometimes we sin intentionally. The Bible lets us know that pride and self-centeredness are at the core of our sin. For many of us, our sin is frustrating because we want to do better. The apostle

Paul expresses his frustration at his own sin in Romans chapter 7, and the rest of us are right beside him.

Fortunately for Christians, God is amazingly forgiving. First John chapter 1 tells us, "If we say we have no sin, we deceive ourselves, and the truth is not in us. If we confess our sins, he is faithful and just to forgive us our sins and to cleanse us from all unrighteousness. If we say we have not sinned, we make him a liar, and his word is not in us." Nehemiah was well aware of God's forgiving nature because he appeals to God to remember His promise if His people returned to Him and kept His commandments. Nehemiah also realized God's mighty power had redeemed His chosen people, and that He would always preserve them. Do you make it a practice in your prayers to confess your sins to God and ask for forgiveness? After you have confessed your sins, do you grab hold of God's promise of forgiveness instead of letting your mind dwell on past sins? Do you remind yourself that God redeemed you through His mighty power through the blood of Jesus Christ?

This aspect of confession of sins and trust in God's forgiveness cannot be overlooked in a kingdom business. We sin against customers, employees, vendors, and partners. We sin against family members. As much as we detest it, and as hard as it is for entrepreneurs and leaders to sometimes admit, we are deeply flawed individuals who are in constant need of God's grace. Fortunately, God is merciful beyond our ability to understand, and this knowledge keeps us moving forward to love and serve Him. It should also encourage us to be gracious and forgiving when other people who impact our business sin against us.

Nehemiah ends his prayer by asking for God's blessing on his request and the actions that he plans to take, and then letting us know he was the cupbearer to the king. The application of verse 11 could be a book in itself for a business owner, but I will try to be as brief as possible without shortchanging the important aspects.

First, Nehemiah reveals that he has a plan of some sort that he intends to act upon. We won't fully know his plan until chapter 2, but we can surmise by what we've read so far that he intends to speak to his employer, the king, about the desperate condition of the Jewish exiles. Keep in mind that God has not audibly spoken to Nehemiah about his kingdom-building business, yet he has decided to do something about a situation that he feels strongly about. Because he was a man who loved God and who was intimately acquainted with God's Word, he was acutely tuned in to the direction of God's Holy Spirit directing Him.

What an amazingly important point this is. Just as God did not audibly speak to Nehemiah, neither does He speak audibly to us today. Nevertheless, we are just like Nehemiah in that God speaks to us through His Word and Spirit, so we know what is right from wrong. We know if our motivations and plans are designed to bring glory to God. Knowing his own motivation to bring glory to God by helping God's people, Nehemiah was confident of God's inner call and responded to Him by moving full speed ahead. He had confidence that what He was about to do was in God's will, and we can have the same confidence if we know we desire to build God's kingdom and give Him glory. That doesn't mean we will always succeed, but it makes us confident knowing we are seeking to please Him.

The second important part of verse 11 was that Nehemiah was willing to give up his comfortable and influential position as the king's cupbearer in order to pursue a dangerous endeavor with no guarantee of success. He could have suggested to the king that someone else go, or that the king form a special committee to investigate the matter. Instead, he decided to be a courageous man of action, willing to make sacrifices to help build the kingdom.

Finally, the most important aspect of verse 11 is that Nehemiah shows he is completely dependent upon God for success. He knows this task is monumental, and a lot of things have to go right for it to succeed. However, he also knows he can lean on the strength of God's almighty power to supply all his needs to get the job done. This is a wonderful picture of a motivated individual like you or me being willing to take enormous, skillful actions while at the same time acknowledging that the success of those actions is wholly dependent upon God.

As we conclude this chapter, please pray about the types of kingdom needs God would have you pursue through your business or the wealth created by it. Somewhere within the kingdom there is a great need that can be addressed by you, and the people with the need may not even know they need what you can provide. Or, they may not have the resources to provide it themselves. This was the case with Nehemiah. The Israelites didn't have the wall, and they were miserable as a result. Some may have known they needed it, while others may never have given it a thought. Nevertheless, they were all made better by one man listening to the Holy Spirit telling him to take action.

As an entrepreneur or business leader, you probably have more leadership experience and skill than the average person, and God wants you to use those gifts for His kingdom. Remember Ephesians 2:10, which we discussed earlier. God has work for you to do that He has prepared beforehand for you to perform. What is His Spirit saying to you, and are you willing to go where He leads?

As you ponder your steps and put together your action plan, remember the various aspects of Nehemiah's prayer, and make it a model prayer. Praise God from an informed knowledge of the Scriptures, confess your sins to Him and acknowledge His mercy and forgiveness, and understand that the success of your plan is completely dependent upon Him. Does what He has given you seem too daunting? Remember Ephesians 3:20: "Now to him who is able to do far more abundantly than all that we ask or think, according to the power at work within us." Remember the power of God's Spirit working in you to do incredible things through your business.

What He has given you may be big and difficult, and may require sacrifice, but through prayer and perseverance, you can do it.

View From the Trenches

Having confidence in God's call is critical to you as a kingdom entrepreneur or business leader. Just as we'll see Nehemiah going through challenging times, it is practically guaranteed that you and your business will as well. Frequently, when situations become difficult, Christians give up by saying, "It must not be God's will for me to do this." Well, that might be true, but think about all the hardships endured by Abraham, Joseph, Moses, Joshua, David, Paul, Peter, and Jesus. None of them had an easy road, but they kept going because they were certain of their calling. This certainty of our calling is what kept us going at Busy Bees during the most difficult times.

Like Nehemiah, we had a driving passion that set the wheels in motion for Busy Bees Christian PreSchool. We see a society that is degenerating morally and rapidly abandoning the God-centered principles of our nation's founding. It disturbs us that we are drifting further and further away from God. This very thing happened to Old Testament Israel, and that is why their nation was split in two and eventually conquered and enslaved. And it can all happen in one generation.

Israel followed God until all the elders of Joshua's generation passed away, then they started worshiping idols within one generation. Why? Probably because no leader rose up in Joshua's place and because parents stopped teaching their children about God. After all, the Promised Land was conquered. Most of their enemies were soundly defeated. Surely, they could ease up a little on their kids so they could have it better than their parents. Bad thinking.

This idea of passing Christ along to the next generation, as well as helping create future leaders, was part of our initial Busy Bees mission. We were discouraged by the government-run schools, with their insistence on not only leaving Christ out of everything, but also their increasing intolerance of anything Christian. Think how crazy this is in light of Proverbs 1:7, which says, "The fear of the Lord is the beginning of knowledge; fools despise wisdom and instruction." Our government schools separate the Creator from creation; therefore, what they teach is foolishness, incomplete knowledge. Yes, many facts they teach are true, but they are taught in a vacuum without reference to their origin.

We think it is tragic that our nation's children are being "educated" without the benefit of seeing how all knowledge relates back to God. One could argue that it is the job of the parents and church to educate children about God and bring all the facts of their government education together under the umbrella of a Christian worldview and life view. We understand that argument, but it doesn't negate the fact that God's Word says learning without also fearing the Lord shows foolishness.

So, putting these thoughts together, we felt God was calling us to help our nation get back on track by spreading the gospel to very young children and their families. Our nation's deteriorating relationship with God and its corrupt educational system became the equivalent to us of the Jewish exiles being in misery and danger. Creating an alternative school system where kids could learn God's Word every day became the wall we wanted to build in order to help bring people back to God.

So, after a lot of prayer, we decided to begin our mission of helping build God's kingdom by creating a for-profit preschool. Neither of our kids had gone to a preschool, so we performed considerable research to find out more about them. We searched our area for locations. We ran financial pro formas and tried to consider everything that could go wrong. We researched preschool curricula and basically did as much preparation as we thought we could prior to getting started.

But the main takeaway was answering God's burning call to help rebuild the broken-down walls of American culture and education, and to help build a foundation of Christianity for the children and families in our part of the country. We felt like we simply had to do something, and being business people, we knew our preschool, Busy Bees, would have to generate a significant amount of profitability in order to fuel the vision, keep it going, and add more schools later on.

Chapter 5

Acting on God's Call:
Nehemiah Chapter 2

But someone will say, "You have faith and I have works."
Show me your faith apart from your works, and I will show
you my faith by my works.

James 2:18

Thinking about a major endeavor such as a change of career or a change in direction for your business, or even a major project, is often an intoxicating experience. As entrepreneurs we imagine all the good things that will happen as a result of our plans. Since we are people of action and not mere philosophers and idea generators, at some point, we come to the moment of truth, the time when we must make that commitment and take those steps. Even when we have prayed, planned, and examined our ideas from what we perceive as every angle, there is that frequently nerve-wracking moment in time when we must begin, heart pounding, realizing there is no turning back. This is what happened to Nehemiah in chapter 2. Let's see how he handled it.

¹In the month of Nisan, in the twentieth year of King Artaxerxes, when wine was before him, I took up the wine and gave it to the king. Now I had not been sad in his presence. ²And the king said to me, "Why is your face sad, seeing

you are not sick? This is nothing but sadness of the heart."
Then I was very much afraid. [3]I said to the king, "Let the
king live forever! Why should not my face be sad, when the
city, the place of my fathers' graves, lies in ruins, and its
gates have been destroyed by fire?" [4]Then the king said to
me, "What are you requesting?" So I prayed to the God of
heaven. [5]And I said to the king, "If it pleases the king, and if
your servant has found favor in your sight, that you send me
to Judah, to the city of my fathers' graves, that I may rebuild
it." [6]And the king said to me (the queen sitting beside him),
"How long will you be gone, and when will you return?" So
it pleased the king to send me when I had given him a time.
[7]And I said to the king, "If it pleases the king, let letters be
given me to the governors of the province Beyond the River,
that they may let me pass through until I come to Judah, [8]and
a letter to Asaph, the keeper of the king's forest, that he may
give me timber to make beams for the gates of the fortress
of the temple, and for the wall of the city, and for the house
that I shall occupy." And the king granted me what I asked,
for the good hand of my God was upon me.

[9]Then I came to the governors of the province Beyond
the River and gave them the king's letters. Now the king had
sent with me officers of the army and horsemen. [10]But when
Sanballat the Horonite and Tobiah the Ammonite servant
heard this, it displeased them greatly that someone had come
to seek the welfare of the people of Israel.

[11]So I went to Jerusalem and was there three days. [12]Then
I arose in the night, I and a few men with me. And I told no
one what my God had put into my heart to do for Jerusalem.
There was no animal with me but the one on which I rode.
[13]I went out by night by the Valley Gate to the Dragon Spring
and to the Dung Gate, and I inspected the walls of Jerusalem
that were broken down and its gates that had been destroyed
by fire. [14]Then I went on to the Fountain Gate and to the
King's Pool, but there was no room for the animal that was
under me to pass. [15]Then I went up in the night by the valley
and inspected the wall, and I turned back and entered by

the Valley Gate, and so returned. [16]And the officials did not know where I had gone or what I was doing, and I had not yet told the Jews, the priests, the nobles, the officials, and the rest who were to do the work.

[17]Then I said to them, "You see the trouble we are in, how Jerusalem lies in ruins with its gates burned. Come, let us build the wall of Jerusalem, that we may no longer suffer derision." [18]And I told them of the hand of my God that had been upon me for good, and also of the words that the king had spoken to me. And they said, "Let us rise up and build." So they strengthened their hands for the good work. [19]But when Sanballat the Horonite and Tobiah the Ammonite servant and Geshem the Arab heard of it, they jeered at us and despised us and said, "What is this thing that you are doing? Are you rebelling against the king?" [20]Then I replied to them, "The God of heaven will make us prosper, and we his servants will arise and build, but you have no portion or right or claim in Jerusalem."

Attracting a Key Investor: Verses 1-8

So far, we know Nehemiah was a man of God with plans to undertake a great work for God. However, he had a few problems, too, which some of you may be able to relate to. He had an excellent full-time job with the king in Shushan, so how could he do this great work in Jerusalem, which was about 800 miles away? By the way, their main transportation was not motorized, so 800 miles was one foot after the other. In addition, he lacked the resources to achieve his objectives. Sound familiar? Despite these apparent obstacles, Nehemiah had a plan that he had been building and praying over for about four months.

The text does not tell us when Nehemiah planned to ask the king for the time off and resources to execute his plan, but we know Nehemiah had planned those things because of how he responded to the king in verses 5 and 7. He may have been praying for God to open a door and show him when to make his request to the king. What we do know is that he was put on the spot by the king at a moment when he may not have been ready. When the king did this, Nehemiah says he was "very much afraid." It was the moment of truth, and his heart was in his throat. The king perceived that Nehemiah was obviously not his normal self, no doubt due to the great burden he was carrying around. No doubt, Nehemiah would have liked to have been in a better mood or had more advance warning of the king's question. Perhaps this was not the way he envisioned bringing this topic to the king. However, God thought it was the right time, so there he was, in front of the king, and very afraid. God's timing doesn't always coincide with ours, so we need to be watching, waiting, and preparing for the time when He opens the doors for us.

Why was Nehemiah so fearful? Years earlier, the same king had issued an order to stop rebuilding the city (Ezra 4:21), so now Nehemiah was asking him to reverse it. He could have had Nehemiah disciplined, demoted, fired, imprisoned, or even executed for making such a request.

With the king's spotlight fully on him, full of fear, what did Nehemiah do? He put his faith in God and proceeded to tell his problem to the king. Rather than act hatefully toward Nehemiah, this pagan king shows kindness to Nehemiah by asking him what he wants. Nehemiah responds characteristically by praying to God, then asking the king to send him to Judah to rebuild the city.

There is much to discuss about this little interchange, and let's focus on Nehemiah's obstacles mentioned above, his relationship with the king, his courage and preparedness in responding to the king, and his trust in God's sovereign hand at work.

You might be locked into a job, like I am, or you may lack the resources to build your kingdom business. Don't let these things hold you back from pursuing the goals God has laid on your heart. Remember, He has all the resources. He owns everything. Think of Nehemiah. He did not let himself be bound by what some might consider constraints. He leveraged his relationship with the king to get both the time and resources he needed. From the world's perspective, how was he able to do this?

It appears that he had an excellent relationship with the king. He had performed his tasks well and had clearly gained the king's confidence. Why else would the king have provided Nehemiah with the resources and autonomy we read about later in the chapter? This is a great example of the benefit of working hard for others, looking out for their best interests, and having integrity in all we do. With these in place, even nonbelievers will be willing to help us reach our goals. Just look at the example of Joseph and Pharaoh in Genesis, or Daniel and Nebuchadnezzar in the book of Daniel.

If you lack time or resources, God has no doubt uniquely positioned you with particular relationships. Think about people with whom have you made relationships of trust and integrity who also possess the things you need to accomplish your kingdom business goals. Surely, God has put someone in your path who either has the resources you need or who knows someone with those resources. Note that resources do not only refer to money. They could be time, skills, knowledge, influence, or any of a number of valuable assets that could benefit your business. In following Nehemiah's example, we need to be willing to pray and ask for the participation of those individuals with needed resources.

Next let's observe that Nehemiah had a great business case prepared and was ready to sell it even under less than ideal circumstances. No doubt, he had gone over this many times in his mind and probably practiced it out loud on a number of occasions. You don't need me to give you a lecture on having a good business case and sales presentation for whatever you want to accomplish. I merely point out for your benefit that this is not a modern invention, nor is it to be viewed as an unsavory business tactic. If a man of God can use it to accomplish kingdom objectives, it might be a good idea for you and me to take note of it.

It is interesting to observe that his presentation may have been more tailored to the king than a superficial inspection might reveal. Notice that Nehemiah used the terms "the city of my fathers" and "Judah" instead of "Jerusalem." Since the king had previously ordered work on the city to cease many years earlier, Nehemiah may have thought it wise to avoid using words that might bring back bad memories to the king. Neither did Nehemiah give the king a theological lecture or a speech on how he needed to repent and be baptized. He spoke about things that the king could easily understand and relate to. The lesson is that the words we use matter a great deal, and tailoring them to the particular individuals we are trying to influence is crucial. Even though God was superintending over this entire endeavor, He uses our practiced skills within small details to help bring about His will.

This brings us to Nehemiah's trust in God's sovereign hand working in the situation. Knowing Scripture as he did, Nehemiah undoubtedly recalled Proverbs 21:1, which says, "The king's heart is a stream of water in the hand of the LORD; he turns it wherever he will." Yes, God reigns supreme even over pagan rulers. So, even if we think someone would never agree to our request, we prayerfully ask anyway because we know nothing is impossible with God. Remember, He does immeasurably, abundantly more than we can ask or think through His power working in us.

After the king had shown an interest by requesting more information, Nehemiah prays once again before making his more detailed request to the king. Let's see if we can get this picture more clearly in our minds. The king and Nehemiah are basically eye to eye, perhaps only several feet away from one another. Nehemiah is being questioned intently by a world leader who happens to be the only person who can assist him with his life's work. The king has opened the door to Nehemiah by asking him a follow-up question, and before he answers, Nehemiah prays. Remember, he said he was very afraid. Maybe he prayed for courage. Perhaps he prayed to be able to quickly recall everything he had been thinking about these past four months. What we can surmise is that Nehemiah didn't drop to his knees in front of the king and begin praying. No, this was a quick prayer, lasting no more than a second or two, done while he was looking at the king. This is a great example of how the power of prayer is available to us at all times, even under the most stressful and time-sensitive situations.

Nehemiah's requests further showed his preparedness by asking for specific resources, such as letters of safe passage and timber from the king's forest. These may seem modest, but keep in mind, the timber had to be transported a great distance. That would take money and manpower. Nevertheless, the fact that Nehemiah made relatively modest and sensible requests instead of asking for silver and gold, or a large army, probably gave the king greater confidence in his cupbearer. Nehemiah was open and honest with the king about how his resources would be used, and they also agreed on a time for Nehemiah's return.

If you are going to ask someone for help with part of your kingdom business, you will need to be at least as prepared as Nehemiah. It is not mentioned here, but Nehemiah probably had a good pro forma estimate of what he thought he would need, as well as an estimate of the time it would take. If we plan to use other people's resources in our business, smart people are not going to give us a never-ending stream of money. They are going to expect a well-thought-out operational and financial plan, and they are going to want to know when they can expect some sort of payback or return on investment. We have to have those things well-thought-out.

Additionally, if we are going to request the help of people with resources, Nehemiah shows us it is helpful to be somewhat reserved and conservative. Only ask for what we think we will truly need. Showing resourcefulness and a spirit of conservation instead of lavishness often will cause others to have more confidence in us.

By asking for letters of safe passage, we see Nehemiah looking ahead at the things that could go wrong, even in the beginning of his kingdom endeavor. Even though you and I can't anticipate everything that can go wrong, it is to our benefit to think of and prepare for as many contingencies as we can, particularly if solving them is dependent upon the resources of an investor or partner. Things such as business licenses, articles of incorporation, complying with the regulatory agencies for your industry, developing a marketing plan, and becoming familiar with human resources law are all examples of the type of advance preparation we need to do to get our kingdom businesses started.

You may have plenty of resources, so these issues may be irrelevant to you from the standpoint of funding a kingdom project or business. This discussion is not to imply that every kingdom business needs an investor of some sort in order to follow a biblical pattern. It simply points out that this is the route Nehemiah took when he himself lacked resources. If you have your own resources, that's great. My question to you in that case would be, Who do you know that has a Nehemiah-like vision, but lacks resources? Can you help them get off the ground by investing in them, assuming their ideas and plans are solid?

A major point of this chapter is that the resources we need are often closer to us than we think. We just may not have thought or prayed through the different options available to us. Your resources could be your current or former employer, a friend of a friend, your church, a vendor, or other business people with whom you have relationships. The key is praying, not being afraid to ask, presenting a well-thought-out business case to someone with whom you have a proven relationship of integrity, and trusting God to supply your needs.

By this point, everything was going Nehemiah's way. Many people would have celebrated and congratulated themselves on being able to make an investor out of the king. They may have reflected on how great their sales presentation was, how slick their words were, or how well their months of planning had worked. This was not how Nehemiah thought. What did he do instead? He acknowledged God's almighty power by saying in verse 8, "And the king granted me what I asked, for the good hand of my God was upon me." When you have major victories in your business, do you gloat, or do you acknowledge God's sovereign power at work in your business? Remember the words of Jesus in John 15:5: "I am the vine; you are the branches. Whoever abides in me and I in him, he it is that bears much fruit, for apart from me you can do nothing."

The Journey Begins: Verses 9-10

The typical flow of a major endeavor, such as the start of a business or launch of a new product line, is to acquire the resources to produce whatever needs to be produced, then to skillfully put those resources to use in a way that creates an excellent return on investment. That's what Nehemiah begins to do in these verses.

Nehemiah had asked for letters from the king in order to give him safe passage along the long and dangerous journey. Evidently, the king was so fond of Nehemiah, and so convinced of the worthiness of his project, that he also sent army officers and cavalry to protect him along the journey. We see that Nehemiah put these resources to use immediately in order to gain official passage through Trans-

Euphrates. No doubt, it was an impressive sight when Nehemiah showed up with army officers, cavalry, and letters of recommendation from one of the most powerful men in the world. Once again, we see God supplying Nehemiah with more than He even asked for.

So far, everything had been going along smoothly for Nehemiah, but in verse 10, we learn that not everyone is happy about the start of this kingdom business. In fact, some people actually had an interest in the Israelites remaining in their current desperate state. Scripture does not say why these two officials, Sanballat and Tobiah, wanted to keep the Israelites in their oppressed state. It probably is not a stretch to think that somehow keeping the Jews down and out led to greater economic or political power for these two men. We don't know how Nehemiah knew about the opposition of Sanballat and Tobiah, but we assume he heard it through the grapevine. Later, Nehemiah will tell us of his direct encounters with these two men as their opposition to him becomes fierce.

Should we really be surprised that Nehemiah encountered opposition so early in his project? As Christians, how can we be surprised by opposition when Jesus Himself was opposed to the point of being betrayed and crucified? From the very beginning of creation, Adam and Eve were opposed by Satan, and the opposition hasn't stopped since. What is behind this opposition? Darkness cannot coexist with light. Evil cannot coexist with good. Darkness and evil must wage war against light and good in order to survive. Evil's intent is to poison and conquer everything in its path. Christians get in its way and throw it off course. Not only that, Romans 8:37 says, "We are more than conquerors." Christ has defeated darkness and evil in an eternal sense, but it is still waging war against God's people.

So please don't expect to go unopposed in your kingdom business. The enemy has great interest in your failure and will wage war against you. If your kingdom business succeeds in helping to spread the gospel by helping others, that will be a major blow against the enemy, and he will work hard against you. Nevertheless, be strong. Recall the words of the great hymn by Martin Luther, "A Mighty Fortress Is Our God." We will discuss opposition in greater detail later, but it is important to note its presence early in Nehemiah's project. If you are just starting your kingdom business, you need to be prepared not only for the normal difficulties encountered with a startup; you need to be equally prepared for the spiritual warfare that is sure to come.

Building a Team in Jerusalem: Verses 11-20

Nehemiah and his military escort finally arrived in Jerusalem. So far, everything was going according to plan. He tells us that he stayed there for three days before setting out at night to survey the wall. He also tells us that he did not mention his plans for Jerusalem to anyone. So for three days, he probably asked a lot of questions about the Jews and found out who some of the key people were, all the while keeping his mission top secret.

Remember, Nehemiah was a stranger to the Jews, even though he was one of them. As far as they knew, he could have been an emissary from the king, sent to spy on them for some unsavory purpose. He couldn't just ride into town telling everyone he was going to save them and expected the people to immediately trust him. I imagine he built some relationships during those three days by encouraging people through God's Word and by telling them of the king's desire to help them.

Likewise, Nehemiah also took time to survey the wall by night. Since he didn't want anyone to know his plan, he had to survey the wall discreetly. Like any good leader, Nehemiah wanted to see as much as possible what he was getting into. He needed to know the extent of the damage to the wall in various places, as well as gain an understanding of places that might be particularly vulnerable to attack from enemies. He was examining the details of the project, not from afar, but from on site. He had put together a lot of great planning from the citadel of Shushan, but planning and pro formas only go so far.

Nehemiah knew he was going to need a large, committed team to get this project completed, and I believe the reason he maintained such secrecy about his desire to rebuild the walls was so that he could be completely informed and come to his team with a well-thought-out plan to get the work done. In addition, he probably anticipated the naysayers, those who might say, "You should see what it's like down at the Fountain Gate. It will be impossible to rebuild that part of the wall." I think he wanted to be able to say, "Yes, I have seen the Fountain Gate, and this is how we're going to approach it." He knew he might only have one shot to assemble a team that bought into his vision, so he took the steps necessary to help the people have confidence in his plan.

Not until you are actually involved in your kingdom business will you fully understand the challenges presented to you. It is very different going from the pro forma world to the real world, and your team is counting on you to fully grasp the real world core issues because they need you to have that understanding in order to lead them. People want to be led, and they are ready to be led. However, they're not stupid. They want to follow someone with a strong vision and an excellent command of the facts. They don't want some pie-in-the-sky blowhard. They want a real person with a clear understanding of the problems and a sensible approach to solving them.

Notice what happened in Nehemiah's case after he had fully examined the situation. He was able to rally the people together and tell them the details of how God had paved the road for them to rebuild the city and put their culture back together. Perhaps during this meeting, he also talked to them about the details of how they would approach working on and defending different parts of the wall. No doubt, he also got their input regarding the capabilities of different team members, how to organize the work force, and even sources of supplies and raw materials they might need.

Based on Nehemiah's detailed and well-thought-out plan, coupled with his enthusiasm and obvious call from God, it is no wonder the people responded enthusiastically. Like I told you, they were ready to be led. God had prepared the way for Nehemiah to put his vision in place by preparing the hearts of the people who would help. Likewise, God will supply you with workers and customers who share your same vision. There are many people who have hearts for God, but who don't know how to put their gifts or desires into action. They are waiting for a visionary leader and entrepreneur like you to provide inspiration and give them a clear path to follow.

At the end of this chapter, we see Nehemiah's chief enemies, Sanballat and Tobiah, taking a more active approach to their opposition. They mocked and ridiculed Nehemiah and the Jews, and in the process made fools of themselves. Nehemiah knew good and well that he was acting on the authority of the king, not rebelling against him. Clearly, this was an attempt to discourage the Israelites from going along with Nehemiah's plan by making them fear reprisals from the king. They, no doubt, knew of Nehemiah's royal military escort as well as his letters of safe passage, so they were intentionally lying in order to weaken the team's motivation.

As I have said, the enemy will stop at nothing to derail your kingdom business, including lies and intimidation. The enemy might even tell lies about you to your employees or customers. Be prepared, but not afraid. You have the King of Kings and Lord of Lords on your side.

Nehemiah responds to his enemies by affirming his faith in God's grace and mercy. He basically says his team is moving forward no matter what they say. Nehemiah and his team are going to pursue their mission no matter what. Psalm 37:1, 3 says it best: "Fret not yourself because of evildoers. . . . Trust in the Lord, and do good." This is what Nehemiah did, and it is what we have tried to do over and over again at Busy Bees Christian PreSchool. I encourage you to do the same. Nehemiah tells them they have no claim, share, or historic right to Jerusalem. He's right. Jerusalem is for God's chosen people, and He promises us we'll get there. That's what we need to remember when our enemies try to intimidate us.

View From the Trenches

From the time we became convinced that God wanted us to open a Christian preschool to the time Busy Bees actually opened seemed like forever. We prayed about locations, curriculum, hiring employees, and whether or not God really wanted us to do this.

After a few years looking for locations and studying the business, we had clear direction from God that He wanted us to buy a four-acre piece of land adjacent to a four-business strip mall. Our thought was that we would sell two acres and use the cash from the sale to build a school on the remaining two acres. It was a great plan, except for the fact that the two acres weren't selling. Cindy and I became discouraged after spending so much time looking for a location, then feeling like we were stalled out, in a holding pattern. After several years of holding the four acres, and paying a sizable chunk of interest each year, we were fed up with the land and just wanted to get rid of it. We thought we had possibly misread everything we thought God had wanted us to do, but we soon learned otherwise.

We had always been praying for it to sell, and just about the time we were at our greatest level of discouragement, God brought a buyer to us who enabled us to realize a large return on the land. Not only did this investor buy our four acres, he also bought the strip center adjacent to it. We had never met this man, but somehow he heard through several contacts that we had been looking for a location for our school. Since he needed tenants for the strip center, he asked if we would like to locate our school in his facility.

This was the equivalent of the king putting Nehemiah on the spot. Our preschool idea had begun to fade away as we languished through the gruesome process of trying to sell the four acres. Suddenly, God rekindled the idea in us through the questioning of this man whom we did not even know. After praying about it, we decided this was God's way of opening the door for us to walk through. Just like with Nehemiah, God put us on the spot, gave us the courage to move forward, and provided us with the cash resources needed to get started.

Like Nehemiah, we were very afraid. We had no experience in this business; had no employees; and had no toys, furnishings, books, or anything else needed to operate the business. Once we signed the lease, there was no turning back, and we were hit with the feeling that we absolutely had to succeed. We were on our way to Jerusalem.

There was a three- or four-month interim period when we were getting the business ready to open. It was equivalent to Nehemiah's time in Jerusalem before actually beginning work on the wall. Some of the most important work we did was to build a team that believed in our vision. I had learned from leading people in the corporate world that imparting a strong vision to your team and reinforcing it frequently is absolutely essential to success; otherwise, people will flounder, lose interest, and go through the motions. Proverbs says, "Without vision the people perish." I have found that as the leader, I have to supply that vision and make sure my employees understand it, believe it, and live it. One of the most critical aspects of this is getting employees to believe in you so that they trust you and your ideas enough to work hard for them each day. To this end, Cindy and I realize that we have to continually build and fuel the confidence of our employees in us personally as well as in our vision for Busy Bees.

What Nehemiah did during his time in Jerusalem prior to starting the wall was to gain that initial trust and buy in. After that, the people saw him exemplify his vision over and over again through his actions. That's the model Cindy and I want our employees to see in us. While we strive to be more consistent in our application of Nehemiah's example, through prayer we have faith that God will help us not only verbalize our vision for Busy Bees, but also live it out in front of our employees.

One thing we know for certain is this: Even though we are in the preschool business, we are really in the people development business. It's the same with the team I lead at the bank, and I have no doubt it's the same in your business. No matter what classification a business falls into, at the end of the day, all business owners are in the people development business. Without focusing outwardly for the benefit of other people, whether they be your customers, employees, or suppliers, your business will not truly be a kingdom business.

How do I know this with such certainty? Simply look at Jesus Christ. He did not come to earth, die on the cross, and rise from the dead to sell more widgets or make more money. His purpose was to develop people for the glory of God. What are His goals in developing us? Romans 12:2 says, "Be transformed by the renewal of your mind." Jesus wants us to be continually transforming, becoming more and more like Him. Ultimately, Romans 8 tells us we will be totally transformed, perfected, when we go to be with Him.

The Bible gives us clear evidence that developing people was always God's plan, and He brought that to completion and fulfillment in Jesus Christ. Look at the example of Nehemiah. His goal, very clearly, was to redevelop the Israelites into a people that worshiped and obeyed God. As part of the process, he had to rebuild Jerusalem, which would help transform them physically and spiritually.

We will develop this idea of people development throughout the remaining chapters of the book. Nehemiah started the process by sharing his vision and calling to his team. We have done this at Busy Bees, and throughout my leadership career, I have succeeded when I have communicated vision frequently in the context of helping my team members better themselves. Conversely, I have had tough times when I have forgotten this important concept.

Chapter 6

The New Team Begins Its Work: Nehemiah Chapter 3

Only let your manner of life be worthy of the gospel of Christ, so that whether I come and see you or am absent, I may hear of you that you are standing firm in one spirit, with one mind striving side by side for the faith of the gospel.

Philippians 1:27

There is hardly a better feeling than being part of a successful, hardworking team that is united around the same goal. Teams like these don't just appear without having outstanding leadership at their core. As we learned in the last chapter, you, the entrepreneur and business leader, have to be that Christ-centered leadership core, intent on helping your employees, customers, and vendors better themselves. It is up to you to develop a well-crafted vision of where the business is going so you can inspire and rally your employees, and convince them that they will be better off by following you.

In addition, you have to create a work plan that is organized, sensible, and efficient. Some might call this an operational strategy. Your employees will have great ideas about how to get the specific tasks accomplished, but remember, it is you who has the big picture plan, and you know how all the work has to fit together. Your employees are focused on the details of executing the plan, so you should not burden them further by placing the development of your operational strategy on their shoulders. You each have different roles on the team, and when everyone recognizes and appreciates those different roles, a kingdom team comes together, one that "stands fast in one spirit, with one mind striving together for the faith of the gospel."

We find these characteristics of a great team here in Nehemiah chapter 3. While at first glance, this chapter may appear to be just a list of people engaged in a construction project in the middle of the desert, I assure you, it is much more. In my opinion, it is one of the most encouraging and instructive chapters in the entire Bible. In it Nehemiah shows us what happened with an energized and united team that believed in his vision and carried it out with a detailed and well-thought-out work plan. Let's read the chapter now.

[1]Then Eliashib the high priest rose up with his brothers the priests, and they built the Sheep Gate. They consecrated it and set its doors. They consecrated it as far as the Tower of the Hundred, as far as the Tower of Hananel. [2]And next to him the men of Jericho built. And next to them Zaccur the son of Imri built.

[3]The sons of Hassenaah built the Fish Gate. They laid its beams and set its doors, its bolts, and its bars. [4]And next to them Meremoth the son of Uriah, son of Hakkoz repaired. And next to them Meshullam the son of Berechiah, son of Meshezabel repaired. And next to them Zadok the son of Baana repaired. [5]And next to them the Tekoites repaired, but their nobles would not stoop to serve their Lord.

[6]Joiada the son of Paseah and Meshullam the son of Besodeiah repaired the Gate of Yeshanah. They laid its beams and set its doors, its bolts, and its bars. [7]And next to them repaired Melatiah the Gibeonite and Jadon the Meronothite, the men of Gibeon and of Mizpah, the seat of the governor of the province Beyond the River. [8]Next to them Uzziel the son of Harhaiah, goldsmiths, repaired. Next to him Hananiah, one of the perfumers, repaired, and they restored Jerusalem as far as the Broad Wall. [9]Next to them Rephaiah the son of Hur, ruler of half the district of Jerusalem, repaired. [10]Next

to them Jedaiah the son of Harumaph repaired opposite his house. And next to him Hattush the son of Hashabneiah repaired. [11]Malchijah the son of Harim and Hasshub the son of Pahath-moab repaired another section and the Tower of the Ovens. [12]Next to him Shallum the son of Hallohesh, ruler of half the district of Jerusalem, repaired, he and his daughters.

[13]Hanun and the inhabitants of Zanoah repaired the Valley Gate. They rebuilt it and set its doors, its bolts, and its bars, and repaired a thousand cubits of the wall, as far as the Dung Gate.

[14]Malchijah the son of Rechab, ruler of the district of Beth-haccherem, repaired the Dung Gate. He rebuilt it and set its doors, its bolts, and its bars.

[15]And Shallum the son of Col-hozeh, ruler of the district of Mizpah, repaired the Fountain Gate. He rebuilt it and covered it and set its doors, its bolts, and its bars. And he built the wall of the Pool of Shelah of the king's garden, as far as the stairs that go down from the city of David. [16]After him Nehemiah the son of Azbuk, ruler of half the district of Beth-zur, repaired to a point opposite the tombs of David, as far as the artificial pool, and as far as the house of the mighty men. [17]After him the Levites repaired: Rehum the son of Bani. Next to him Hashabiah, ruler of half the district of Keilah, repaired for his district. [18]After him their brothers repaired: Bavvai the son of Henadad, ruler of half the district of Keilah. [19]Next to him Ezer the son of Jeshua, ruler of Mizpah, repaired another section opposite the ascent to the armory at the buttress. [20]After him Baruch the son of Zabbai repaired another section from the buttress to the door of the house of Eliashib the high priest. [21]After him Meremoth the son of Uriah, son of Hakkoz repaired another section from the door of the house of Eliashib to the end of the house of Eliashib. [22]After him the priests, the men of the surrounding area, repaired. [23]After them Benjamin and Hasshub repaired opposite their house. After them Azariah the son of Maaseiah, son of Ananiah repaired beside his own house. [24]After him

Binnui the son of Henadad repaired another section, from the house of Azariah to the buttress [25]and to the corner. Palal the son of Uzai repaired opposite the buttress and the tower projecting from the upper house of the king at the court of the guard. After him Pedaiah the son of Parosh [26]and the temple servants living on Ophel repaired to a point opposite the Water Gate on the east and the projecting tower. [27]After him the Tekoites repaired another section opposite the great projecting tower as far as the wall of Ophel.

[28]Above the Horse Gate the priests repaired, each one opposite his own house. [29]After them Zadok the son of Immer repaired opposite his own house. After him Shemaiah the son of Shecaniah, the keeper of the East Gate, repaired. [30]After him Hananiah the son of Shelemiah and Hanun the sixth son of Zalaph repaired another section. After him Meshullam the son of Berechiah repaired opposite his chamber. [31]After him Malchijah, one of the goldsmiths, repaired as far as the house of the temple servants and of the merchants, opposite the Muster Gate, and to the upper chamber of the corner. [32]And between the upper chamber of the corner and the Sheep Gate the goldsmiths and the merchants repaired.

The Value of Kingdom Workers

Notice that chapter 3 makes no mention about extraordinary superstars with advanced degrees from the finest universities. Not that there's anything wrong with fine universities and advanced degrees, but they are not necessary to accomplish great things for God with a kingdom team. Instead, Nehemiah tells us about the contributions of hardworking people operating within a plan, or system, that gave them clear objectives and allowed them to produce measurable results. Their tasks were very well-defined, something that gave them precise goals to focus on.

These people came from diverse backgrounds and skills, as your employees do, but they banded together under Nehemiah's unifying vision of rebuilding the city so they could have safety, economic prosperity, and a sanctuary where they could worship the Lord. Even though building walls was not their primary occupation or trade, they made sacrifices and did what needed to be done to help their kingdom team.

It is very instructive that the names of these hardworking team members are written in the Bible, forever to be remembered by anyone who reads this part of God's Word. Even though they were not leaders or superstars, God took note of their work and let everyone know how much He appreciated their work by memorializing it forever in His Word. What they did seems like small, detailed work, hardly the kind that anyone should take note of, especially God. But God doesn't operate that way. Romans 12, 1 Corinthians 12, and Ephesians 4 all tell us about the different gifts God has given the individual members of the body of Christ. In those passages, it is clear that each of us is designed to have different, but important, contributions to make in order to help build the kingdom.

Just like the people in Nehemiah's day, your employees are performing valuable kingdom tasks for your kingdom business, whether they are selling products, performing janitorial work, or keeping your books. They may not have the vision or leadership skills you have, but your vision can never materialize without them. We see in Nehemiah's example that not every person did the same or equal work. Nevertheless, God wrote their names in His Word. Similarly, God values the efforts your employees make for His kingdom.

Since we will discuss the theme of developing people within the context of your kingdom business, it is worthwhile to consider recognition. As we have seen, God recognized these people not by money or promotions, but simply by holding their achievements up high for all the world to see. Complimenting people for a job well done, along with letting their fellow team members and customers know how much they are appreciated, is an inexpensive, yet powerful, form of developing people and keeping them motivated to do their best.

Your employees may get discouraged from time to time, thinking the minute details of their jobs are not having an impact for God's kingdom. It is important for you, as the leader and visionary, to remind them how important their job is both to your business as well as to God's kingdom. It is not hard to take time to read a simple passage of Scripture with them, perhaps one having to do with spiritual gifts mentioned above. As the big picture person, it also should be easy for you to reaffirm their importance to your company by showing them how their contribution is absolutely essential for everything else to operate smoothly.

Why is this simple form of recognition so hard for us to do as leaders? Perhaps because we are very driven to get our own work done and keep the tasks and work flowing smoothly. I am guilty of forgetting this, and it is complete foolishness to do so. Not only does it make the business run better, but it also is the Christlike thing to do. Think about the example of Jesus when He spoke with the Canaanite woman in Matthew 15:28. He said to her, "O woman, great is your faith! Be it done for you as you desire." What a great compliment from the Savior of the world. Again in Matthew 25:31-40, we are told that Jesus will publicly recognize those who follow Him. As Christians, we publicly praise God and claim Christ as our Savior. That is a great compliment to Him, as it recognizes the work He has done on our behalf, and this gives Him great honor and glory.

Suffice it to say that if we are to build a kingdom business with a kingdom team, we must follow the example of the King by showing sincere appreciation as well as private and public recognition not only to the King, but also to the people who are doing His work for our businesses.

The Value of Meaningful, Well-organized Work

We have seen from this chapter of Nehemiah that he combined meaningful and organized work processes and tasks with the highest form of recognition. Not only does every member on your team want to be recognized by you for a job well done; every member also wants to have meaningful work, to know his work matters to the kingdom. In order for this to happen, you have to think through and create a well-defined organizational plan, listing all the tasks that need to be done, how they should be done, and who should do them. Michael Gerber's excellent book *The E-Myth Revisited* does a sensational job of helping you think through and develop an operational strategy and the subsequent positions and tasks that flow out of it. We won't cover that ground here, but please read that book as well as Gerber's other ones. They are enlightening and helpful.

What I do want to focus on for a few moments is the issue of significant work.

Let's first talk about the need to feel as though their contribution matters. This is contingent upon your having constructed a meaningful vision that your employees believe in, as well as systems that enable your vision to come to life. If you have done a good job thinking through and developing these steps, you will have created important and meaningful work for you and your employees to perform. They will know and understand what purpose their work serves as well as why it is done in a particular way. Let's look at some examples of this from Busy Bees.

View From the Trenches

At Busy Bees, our teachers are well-acquainted with the special-ized purpose of the school, and they all buy into it. We have a particular curriculum that we use that we know does an excellent job supporting our mission and processes. We use specific types of structure in order to ensure our goals are met.

Based on the training and reinforcement we give, there is never a doubt in the teacher's mind that her job is important. She knows beyond a shadow of a doubt that her instruction of students and the way she conducts herself will play a huge role in what the children and parents think and believe about Jesus. She knows her work has the potential to have a lifetime impact on the families she serves, some of who may not know any other Christians besides her. In addition, her satisfaction is increased when she sees and understands her results are superior because she has used the tools and structure we have developed to help her be successful.

Let me share a real-life example with you. In addition to knowing the vision and mission for the school, each teacher has created a purpose, vision, and mission statement for her classroom that is consistent with those for the overall school. Following Gerber's pattern, they have broken out the elements of their mission state-ment and created classroom systems and procedures to measure their progress. As part of this process, the teachers also made operations manuals for each classroom, which will allow any new teacher to come into the room and know where to jump in.

You can see where this system would be helpful not only for keeping the teachers focused and engaged in their work, but also for helping new teachers assimilate into the school. Even more powerfully, if the Lord allows us to create more schools, the new schools will not have to start from scratch.

As your kingdom business grows and changes, it is critical for you, the leader, to help change the work of your employees so it will continue to be important. You will need to restructure positions, create new ones, and eliminate others. Making sure to provide the right training to adapt to these changes is key, and a strong leader will be thinking of those training needs ahead of time, rather than relying upon employees to always notify you when they need new training. After all, they may not even realize that they need new training. They may unknowingly be depending on outdated skills.

Here is a pitfall to beware of: As you go through the year, your employees have a tendency to forget about the relevance of their work unless you develop a way to continually remind them. Not that they do this intentionally, it's just that things can become routine unless you as their leader keep things in front of them. For example, in our weekly staff meeting, where each person discusses his goals for the week, I frequently make an effort to point out how a particular aspect of an employee's project impacts the overall scope of what we are trying to achieve. That keeps everyone informed and reminded of where we're going.

One more critical part of the meaningful work equation is the 80/20 rule. You've got to realize that in any job, 80 percent of the results are accomplished through 20 percent of the activities. To learn more about this, I recommend an excellent book by Richard Koch called *The 80/20 Individual*. While this is a relatively well-known principle, few people or companies I have been associated with have actually figured out how to apply it.

It's up to you to lead your team members in this thinking because you have to help them prioritize their work so they can focus more of their time on the work that makes the most significant impact. This won't happen without your thinking not only about your own work, but about the work of your employees as well. The more you can understand the things that create the greatest amount of value in your business, the more you can help your employees direct their work to the things that will bring the most success and satisfaction to them. Your employees will be happy in their work if you are crystal clear on the most important parts of your business, and then help them use their time and skills to accomplish those parts instead of wasting their precious time on lesser tasks.

While the 80/20 principle is fairly easy to understand, it is not always easy to apply. At Busy Bees, we can have a tendency to slip into performing tasks that create little value, whether it be in the classroom or in our marketing. It takes constant vigilance, information, measuring, and persistence to keep our entire team focused on the most important aspects of our business. One major success we have had with this principle is in the area of expense reduction. We have made a major focus out of eliminating waste in our expenses, and by identifying and focusing on the most valuable tasks, we have become profitable with sixty-five children, whereas we had previously lost money when our enrollment was ten to fifteen students higher.

Finally, since Nehemiah publicly recognized the contributions of his kingdom team, I feel obligated to do the same. It has taken a lot of work to build an excellent team, but we feel we have achieved that at Busy Bees Christian PreSchool. Cindy and I are grateful for the outstanding contributions of the following people: Cindy McClymonds Sr., our COO; Fred McClymonds, CFO; Samantha Sisemore, director; Judy Stark, cook; and our teachers, Siena, Beckie, Kim, Amanda, Hannah, Tiffany, Rhonda, and Megan. Your contributions to the lives of the children and parents we serve is a blessing to them and us and a sweet-smelling aroma to God.

Chapter 7

The Kingdom Team Faces Opposition: Nehemiah Chapter 4

Count it all joy, my brothers, when you meet trials of various kinds, for you know that the testing of your faith produces steadfastness. And let steadfastness have its full effect, that you may be perfect and complete, lacking in nothing.

James 1:2-4

My favorite college football coach is Jim Tressel of the Ohio State Buckeyes. I highly recommend you read his book titled *The Winner's Manual.* If you are a college football fan, you will love the book. However, even if you do not like football, you will benefit from it. Coach Tressel writes about many life lessons beyond football, and one of those lessons is that he says he always learns more from losses than from victories.

Coach Tressel's statement is consistent with one of Scripture's greatest truths: We learn and grow the most in times of trial and adversity. Why is that? James 1:2-4 says that our faith gets tested during these times. That means we are forced to pray and trust in God's promises. These are often times when we understand how fully dependent we are on God's strength, love, and guidance. Not only do we have to pray, but James tells us we also have to be patient and persevere.

Praying, waiting, and persevering are characteristics of all kingdom entrepreneurs. Consider the trials and adversity faced by Joshua. The Bible says he conquered thirty-one kings in all. Think about the daily grind of going into battle with a bunch of filthy, sweaty soldiers, having to lead them when his bones ached, when he was mentally and spiritually weary. Nevertheless, he fought the enemy day after day, year after year. Joshua prayed, waited on the Lord, and persevered. You and I are called to the same daily battle, which will last our entire lifetime on earth. And guess what? Your kingdom business is in the battle. This fact is emphasized to us in Ephesians 6, where the apostle Paul tells us to put on the full armor of God so we may be able to withstand the enemy's attacks, which are sure to come.

Trials come in various forms for you and your business. They can be from difficult employees, customers, or suppliers. They could come from hostile local, state, or federal regulators. It might be that your cash flow isn't what it needs to be and you are having difficulty meeting payroll or paying a bank loan. You might be struggling with a marketing plan, or with implementing a new technology. Maybe demand within your industry is drying up and you need to reinvent your business or yourself. Or maybe like Nehemiah, there are enemies of Christ who have a vested interest in your failure. It could be for political or economic reasons, or it could be the fact that darkness hates the light.

One thing is sure, and that is the wonderful, comforting words of Hebrews 4:15-16 are as true today as the day they were written. Listen to these: "For we do not have a high priest who is unable to sympathize with our weaknesses, but one who in every respect has been tempted as we are, yet without sin. Let us then with confidence draw near to the throne of grace, that we may receive mercy and find grace to help in time of need." Jesus is that High Priest, and we have access to Him at all times. Nehemiah knew this and fled to the throne of grace when confronted with adversity. Let's examine this chapter more closely, and then apply it to your business.

[1]Now when Sanballat heard that we were building the wall, he was angry and greatly enraged, and he jeered at the

Jews. [2]And he said in the presence of his brothers and of the army of Samaria, "What are these feeble Jews doing? Will they restore it for themselves? Will they sacrifice? Will they finish up in a day? Will they revive the stones out of the heaps of rubbish, and burned ones at that?" [3]Tobiah the Ammonite was beside him, and he said, "Yes, what they are building— if a fox goes up on it he will break down their stone wall!" [4]Hear, O our God, for we are despised. Turn back their taunt on their own heads and give them up to be plundered in a land where they are captives. [5]Do not cover their guilt, and let not their sin be blotted out from your sight, for they have provoked you to anger in the presence of the builders.

[6]So we built the wall. And all the wall was joined together to half its height, for the people had a mind to work.

[7]But when Sanballat and Tobiah and the Arabs and the Ammonites and the Ashdodites heard that the repairing of the walls of Jerusalem was going forward and that the breaches were beginning to be closed, they were very angry. [8]And they all plotted together to come and fight against Jerusalem and to cause confusion in it. [9]And we prayed to our God and set a guard as a protection against them day and night.

[10]In Judah it was said, "The strength of those who bear the burdens is failing. There is too much rubble. By ourselves we will not be able to rebuild the wall." [11]And our enemies said, "They will not know or see till we come among them and kill them and stop the work." [12]At that time the Jews who lived near them came from all directions and said to us ten times, "You must return to us." [13]So in the lowest parts of the space behind the wall, in open places, I stationed the people by their clans, with their swords, their spears, and their bows. [14]And I looked and arose and said to the nobles and to the officials and to the rest of the people, "Do not be afraid of them. Remember the Lord, who is great and awesome, and fight for your brothers, your sons, your daughters, your wives, and your homes."

[15]When our enemies heard that it was known to us and that God had frustrated their plan, we all returned to the wall,

each to his work. [16]From that day on, half of my servants worked on construction, and half held the spears, shields, bows, and coats of mail. And the leaders stood behind the whole house of Judah, [17]who were building on the wall. Those who carried burdens were loaded in such a way that each labored on the work with one hand and held his weapon with the other. [18]And each of the builders had his sword strapped at his side while he built. The man who sounded the trumpet was beside me. [19]And I said to the nobles and to the officials and to the rest of the people, "The work is great and widely spread, and we are separated on the wall, far from one another. [20]In the place where you hear the sound of the trumpet, rally to us there. Our God will fight for us."

[21]So we labored at the work, and half of them held the spears from the break of dawn until the stars came out. [22]I also said to the people at that time, "Let every man and his servant pass the night within Jerusalem, that they may be a guard for us by night and may labor by day." [23]So neither I nor my brothers nor my servants nor the men of the guard who followed me, none of us took off our clothes; each kept his weapon at his right hand.

I don't blame you a bit if you became angry reading this chapter. After all, the Jews were minding their own business, rebuilding their city under the orders of the king. Then Sanballat and Tobiah reappeared on the scene. Nehemiah introduced us to them in chapter 2 as people who mocked the efforts of the Jews, insinuating they were rebelling against the king. As they saw work on the wall progressing, with Nehemiah's kingdom team working together enthusiastically, they were enraged. Initially, they expressed their rage by mocking and insulting the Jews, but eventually, their anger took on a more deadly approach as they planned a military operation to attack and kill the Jews to prevent the work from continuing.

The Bible doesn't tell us why these men hated the Jews so much, or why they wanted the rebuilding of the city to fail. We're told they were leaders in some capacity, so we might guess they had political or economic interests in keeping the Jews in a subservient state.

Evidently, Jerusalem was in the middle of a major trade route, so these individuals may have controlled this trade route and may have felt they would lose that control to the Jews if they were allowed to become more organized and powerful.

The fact that these men rose up against the kingdom builders should come as no surprise. From the very beginning of human history, God's people have been doing battle against His enemies. Consider the following examples: Satan's attack and deception of Adam and Eve; Pharaoh's persecution of God's people and his unwillingness to let them leave Egypt; Haman's hatred of the Jews in the book of Esther; the persecution of the apostles and their followers in the New Testament; and the most heinous attack of all, the execution of Jesus Christ.

The one basic reason people rise in opposition to Christianity is this: Their mind-set is darkness, or evil, and the mind-set of a Christian is light, or holiness. That comes right out of John chapter 1. The first part of 1 Corinthians gives us more detail on this difference in mind-set. To the non-Christian, the gospel is foolishness. To the Christian, the world's wisdom without Christ is foolishness. These two mind-sets cannot peacefully coexist. God's enemies are never content to passively tolerate Christians. In fact, they are incapable of doing this since there is no such thing as a neutral person. All of Scripture tells us we are either for God or against Him.

The lesson is this: Expect to be challenged in your kingdom business. We have already established that your business is God's instrument to help build His kingdom. It is not neutral, and while you and your team are rebuilding that part of the wall He has called you to work on, you pose a threat to the enemy. Someone out there has an interest in keeping the walls where they are, destroyed and on the ground. You might not know who they are, and when you discover their identity, you might be surprised. You also may not know when they might launch their attacks, but note that in Nehemiah's case, it was after the Jews had experienced some success. Why would an enemy attack someone or something that was not successfully helping build God's kingdom? Therefore, as the leader, you need to have your eyes open, maintaining vigilance. Let's continue to analyze Nehemiah's situation and his response to it.

As the threats of Sanballat and Tobiah become known to the Jews, the team became frightened and demoralized. Their collective attitude went from highly motivated to thinking their task was impossible. The effects of these threats were physical as well as emotional. We read that the strength of the workers was giving out. Were they really getting weak from the labor itself, or was this physical weakness a result of the stressful conditions in which they found themselves working? I think you and I know the answer.

What was Nehemiah's response to all this? Did he try to ignore it, pretending it didn't exist or wasn't real? Did he try to negotiate with them or make peace in some way? No, he didn't do any of those things. Nehemiah recognized evil for what it is and didn't try to ignore it or negotiate with it. Instead, he gives us the perfect model to help us deal with adversity in our own kingdom businesses. He shows his normal pattern of prayer, followed by clear, well-thought-out action designed to boost the morale of his team members and enhance their ability to meet the threat.

The first time Nehemiah heard of the threat, he prayed and continued the work. When the wall got to about half its designed height and the breaches in it began to close, the enemy's threats became more intense, and the morale of the workers declined significantly. Maybe Nehemiah did not initially realize what these threats would lead to and how destructive they would be to his team. Or, after his first prayer, maybe he felt God leading him to take a watch-and-see position, watching the enemy carefully to see if the rhetoric escalated.

When talk of attack and murder began to filter back to Nehemiah and his team, he realized it was time for him to step up with a stronger defense against the threats. So after leading his team in prayer, he set up a continuous watch against the enemies.

After Judah's report of the diminishing strength and morale of the workers, Nehemiah knew it was time to go to full battle stations. He strategically positioned his people at the weakest parts of the wall and organized them by families, for whom they would be most likely to fight the hardest. In addition to positioning his team to fight the hardest and at the areas of greatest vulnerability, he also encouraged them by telling them not to be afraid of the enemy, to remember the strength and might of the Lord, and to fight for their families.

After all this preparation, something interesting happened: God's enemies decided to call off their attack. Nehemiah credits God by saying He had brought the plans of Sanballat and Tobiah to nothing. So what did Nehemiah do next? The very thing you and I will do, which is to get back to work. Despite God's deliverance from this threat, Nehemiah did not view the threat as being gone forever. He thought his enemies might return, so he made adjustments to the way his people worked. Some worked, while some defended, and a warning system was developed. He took additional precautions to safeguard the people and their work, and reminded them that God would fight for them.

Why was Nehemiah always so confident that God would fight for his people? Remember, this man was a serious student of God's Word, just as you and I need to be in order to build a successful kingdom business. As a student, he recalled all the times from Abraham through David when God came to the defense of His people.

To this point, Psalm 2:1-2 says, "Why do the nations rage and the peoples plot in vain? The kings of the earth set themselves, and the rulers take counsel together, against the Lord and against his Anointed." And what is God's response? Psalm 2:4 says, "He who sits in the heavens laughs; the Lord holds them in derision." Nehemiah knew from the Bible how strong and faithful God was, and he based his leadership strategy squarely on this fact.

Brothers and sisters, fellow kingdom business builders, I hope none of us face the extreme difficulties encountered by Nehemiah. However, all of us know the quickest way to stir up the enemy is to take a firm stand for the Prince of Peace. That's what our kingdom businesses are designed to do, so it would be unwise for us to not prepare for opposition.

We need to be prepared, but not afraid, and ask ourselves some difficult questions. Do we know where our areas of greatest vulnerability are, and have we taken precautions to protect them? They could be computer passwords, building security systems, accounting systems, intellectual property, trademarks, or valuable people or physical assets. It is important for each of us to assess our risks and take action to protect ourselves. In addition, we need to stay attentive to the moods of our people as well as their capabilities. In keeping with the spirit of being in the people development business, building up our employees in Christ helps prepare them for attacks and helps sustain your business through tough times.

Nehemiah paints us a clear portrait of faith, prayer, and action. He provides us with a simple, but effective, model we can incorporate within our own leadership strategy. Using the lessons Nehemiah taught us in this chapter, let's look at some applications in "View From the Trenches."

<u>View From the Trenches</u>

I don't consider myself a paranoid person, and I don't spend a lot of time thinking or worrying about who is out to get me or Busy Bees. But just because I don't worry about these things doesn't mean I don't pray about them and take precautions. While we haven't yet encountered the equivalent of Sanballat or Tobiah, we have been about as close as we want to get to them on multiple occasions. These events have taught us to be both cautious and prepared.

One of the things we've learned to do is to try to anticipate where we might have potential problems. For us, our three main potential sources of attack are employees, customers, and state regulators. That's not to say people can't rise up from other places, but those are our three main areas of exposure.

So far, we have had good success with the state regulators because we have made a point to build good relationships and obey the laws. We take a very proactive approach to reporting any potential problems, and they seem to appreciate that. That doesn't mean we might never come across a rogue state employee who doesn't like Christians, but we will continue to focus on maintaining a current understanding of the rules and actively teaching them in our school.

We have also had a great deal of success with our customers, although a few have turned ugly when we had to "fire" their kids. That's right, we fire three-year-olds. Frequently, a child's behavioral problems will disrupt the classroom for weeks and create an unpleasant atmosphere for the other students as well as the teacher. We have found it much more beneficial for everyone if we step in early and remove the habitually misbehaving child. Of course, it's always the fault of the parents, since they almost always refuse to take accountability for disciplining and controlling their children. When we have to tell someone they can no longer attend Busy Bees, it can lead to emotional flare-ups, which sometimes leave parents raging for weeks or months. Despite the wrath we know we will incur from the parent, combined with the loss of revenue, we have to make the tough calls and disenroll some children whose behavior cannot be controlled.

The only other type of trouble we had with a parent was when someone made verbal and physical threats to an employee. At that point, I immediately intervened on behalf of the employee by confronting the parent and setting up ground rules that would make it difficult for them to continue attending the school.

By far, the main area through which attacks have come has been with employees. Cindy and I have been amazed at the number of employees who have claimed the name of Christ in their interviews, but became anything but Christian when they didn't get their way with decisions relating to pay, promotions, work hours, or time off. Even though these occasions could be the topic of an entire book, I will spare you the gory details and get right to the point: It is difficult to know how someone is going to react when things don't go their way, so we have learned to build systems that limit the exposure of our operation. These systems are both offensive and defensive in nature.

From an offensive standpoint, we try to hire good people from the beginning, and since we are a religious school, we can ask questions about faith and practice during the interview process. We also try to help employees build their faith by providing an optional weekly Bible study, praying and discussing Scripture passages during our team meetings, and encouraging each person to be in daily prayer about his or her job and the children the person serves. We let employees know that since they are doing the Lord's work for the next generation, Satan is going to target them. That's why we try to build them up in Christ as well as encourage them to attend church.

In our team meetings, we do a fair amount of training and place frequent emphasis on our vision, mission, and core values. Finally, our director and I have one-on-one sessions with each employee to show interest in each employee, answer questions, help the person improve his or her performance, listen to concerns, and understand his or her prayer needs.

While none of these activities will change anyone's heart, they plant and water seeds, and give God an opportunity to work in the hearts of our employees as they hear His Word and see it lived out. I'm sure we can do more, but the important point is we are trying to build up our people in Christ so they are able to withstand the daily assault of Satan and the world.

From a defensive standpoint, we try to protect our operation by doing things such as video recording all the activities in the school, requiring security card entrance to the classroom areas, limiting access to marketing and financial systems, and maintaining careful documentation of all customer and employee records. In fact, from our experience, the two areas of greatest potential weakness and risk have been documenting customer and employee records, and maintaining accurate financial records. Several times we have been challenged legally by customers and employees with complaints against us, and in each instance, we were able to prove our compliance with the law simply by the fact that we keep good records.

From a financial standpoint, early on, we realized we had potentially enormous exposure in the collection of tuition. On many occasions, particular employees simply were not collecting tuition if they felt a customer had a legitimate excuse not to pay it. It sounds unthinkable to you and me, but employees can feel this way for a number of reasons. One rationalization is since it is a Christian organization, and Jesus said to give to the poor, we should just let people come without paying if they are having a difficult time. It sounds good in theory until rent and payroll have to be paid. The second rationalization, a bit more sinister, is that you, the business owner, are getting rich off the backs of these employees and customers, all in the name of Christ, so you should be able to give these poor people a break if they can't pay. Now, you or I may choose to give away some of our services for free on occasion, but for the most part, we must get paid for our services or go out of business. Not all employees appreciate this fact, so we have learned to create a system of checks and balances, which closely monitors the flow of funds into and out of Busy Bees.

Of course, our number one weapon against the enemy's attacks is prayer. We pray for our employees and the children and families they serve. We pray that God would lead the children and families to salvation in Christ, and we pray that God would give the employees spiritual growth and a strong relationship with Christ and each other so they can have a strong witness to each other and to our customers. We pray for the safety of the children, the accomplishment of our vision, the glorification of God through our business, and for its financial success. I started this section by stating that we don't worry, but are vigilant. The reason we don't worry is because we can go to God in prayer, knowing He hears us and cares for His people. We find comfort in Him, and that's why we know we can do the right things and make the tough, unpopular, decisions. We know we have to please Him first and live up to His standards as much as we possibly can. If we do this, He will take care of the rest. We have always had success with this approach. God has not one time let us down.

Chapter 8

The Kingdom Team Suffers Internal Strife: Nehemiah Chapter 5

But if you bite and devour one another, watch out that you are not consumed by one another.

Galatians 5:15

One of Satan's main tools in fighting against Christians is to turn them against each other so they fall into sin and become laughingstocks to the world. We witness this strategy with the very first sin Adam and Eve committed by allowing Satan to turn them against God. Because of our tendency to turn against each other, Jesus tells us to love one another, and the apostle Paul tells us to be of one mind and to submit to one another. Instead of biting and devouring one another, Paul tells us to bear one another's burdens, to help each other out in difficult times.

Against this backdrop, we approach Nehemiah chapter 5. This chapter is every business leader's nightmare because it shows us what can be the quick demise of any company—internal strife. If our employees are not united by their commitment to our vision, their sense of responsibility to each other, and their passion for Christ, there is a good chance our businesses will suffer great inefficiencies as a result of internal disagreements and lack of teamwork. Nehemiah encountered these types of difficulties in chapter 5. Let's read the Scripture, and then examine the model Nehemiah has laid out for us.

[1]Now there arose a great outcry of the people and of their wives against their Jewish brothers. [2]For there were those who said, "With our sons and our daughters, we are many. So let us get grain, that we may eat and keep alive." [3]There were also those who said, "We are mortgaging our fields, our vineyards, and our houses to get grain because of the famine." [4]And there were those who said, "We have borrowed money for the king's tax on our fields and our vineyards. [5]Now our flesh is as the flesh of our brothers, our children are as their children. Yet we are forcing our sons and our daughters to be slaves, and some of our daughters have already been enslaved, but it is not in our power to help it, for other men have our fields and our vineyards."

[6]I was very angry when I heard their outcry and these words. [7]I took counsel with myself, and I brought charges against the nobles and the officials. I said to them, "You are exacting interest, each from his brother." And I held a great assembly against them [8]and said to them, "We, as far as we are able, have bought back our Jewish brothers who have been sold to the nations, but you even sell your brothers that they may be sold to us!" They were silent and could not find a word to say. [9]So I said, "The thing that you are doing is not good. Ought you not to walk in the fear of our God to prevent the taunts of the nations our enemies? [10]Moreover, I and my brothers and my servants are lending them money and grain. Let us abandon this exacting of interest. [11]Return to them this very day their fields, their vineyards, their olive orchards, and their houses, and the percentage of money, grain, wine, and oil that you have been exacting from them." [12]Then they said, "We will restore these and require nothing from them. We will do as you say." And I called the priests and made them swear to do as they had promised. [13]I also shook out the fold of my garment and said, "So may God shake out every man from his house and from his labor who does not keep

this promise. So may he be shaken out and emptied." And all the assembly said "Amen" and praised the LORD. And the people did as they had promised.

[14]Moreover, from the time that I was appointed to be their governor in the land of Judah, from the twentieth year to the thirty-second year of Artaxerxes the king, twelve years, neither I nor my brothers ate the food allowance of the governor. [15]The former governors who were before me laid heavy burdens on the people and took from them for their daily ration[16] forty shekels of silver. Even their servants lorded it over the people. But I did not do so, because of the fear of God. [16]I also persevered in the work on this wall, and we acquired no land, and all my servants were gathered there for the work. [17]Moreover, there were at my table 150 men, Jews and officials, besides those who came to us from the nations that were around us. [18]Now what was prepared at my expense for each day was one ox and six choice sheep and birds, and every ten days all kinds of wine in abundance. Yet for all this I did not demand the food allowance of the governor, because the service was too heavy on this people. [19]Remember for my good, O my God, all that I have done for this people.

A No-nonsense Approach to Confrontation

We see from the opening verses that times were exceedingly difficult for many of the people. The famine was so great that they had to mortgage their homes and fields at usurious interest rates in order to acquire food. Even worse, their children were sold into slavery by their fellow Jews because the poor people could not pay their debts. This is in conflict with God's law.

So instead of showing love and lending freely, as Jesus commands, the wealthier Jews decided to make money off of the impoverished situation of the poorer Jews. While Jesus wants us to show compassion to the poor, these Jews saw the poverty of their countrymen as an opportunity to make themselves wealthier.

This situation was clearly incompatible with the unified effort needed to rebuild the wall and city. Remember, Nehemiah was engaged in a kingdom business designed to restore God's people to a right relationship with Him and with each other. The construction project was merely a means of achieving that goal. So it is possible that the construction could have continued, but the people would not have been united in their love and passion for God and each other. They would have had a nice wall and city, but it would have all been for naught.

Likewise, your kingdom business is about more than the products you produce. Your business is a living organism of sorts whose individual and aggregated parts are meant to bring glory to God. Since it is a piece of the church, or body of Christ, to a large extent, it can be a discipling factory if you lead it well. This is part of the people development business mentioned earlier. However, internal divisiveness emanating from pride, jealousy, and selfishness can arise in any organization, just as it did with Nehemiah's team.

This type of internal strife can happen even in a kingdom business with a strong leader like Nehemiah. It has certainly happened in our business when coworkers have not treated each other with the type of courtesy and respect that should be displayed between Christians. Purely and simply, if Satan can't destroy your business and demoralize your work force by outside enemies, he will use indwelling sin to try to turn your team members against each other and against you. There are a number of ways this can happen, including jealousies arising from workers having different salaries, excessive pride being displayed over a promotion or accolade, the feeling that a coworker is not fulfilling his responsibilities, and gossip being spread among team members about the personal lives of other employees.

These types of things happen most frequently when your people turn their focus off of Christ and onto themselves. Unfortunately, this self-centered focus characterizes all of us, not just our employees. No one is immune to it. As the leader, hopefully you realize and adjust to the fact that your needs must come secondary to the needs of your customers and employees. This requires prayer and humility on your part. Nevertheless, your employees may not actively be practicing this all the time, and this is when situations can get heated.

What did Nehemiah do when he learned of this situation? At first, he said he became very angry. As we would expect from him, he says he pondered this situation, and then addressed it. This is one of the few instances when he does not say he prayed before he acted. Maybe he was praying as he was pondering. The main point is that he thought about it before acting and potentially doing or saying something to make it worse.

We get the feeling that Nehemiah acted in a very calculating way. He called a large meeting and addressed the issue in a very clear and direct manner. He did not try to gloss over any of the sins or try to protect the feelings of the offenders. Remember, the people committing these sins were rich and powerful people. Nehemiah probably needed them on his team, and he may have taken a great risk in confronting them openly and directly.

It is very important that Nehemiah actually did take action instead of letting this situation continue and potentially worsen. Consider the two motivations for his action. First, he realized the project was in jeopardy if this situation was allowed to continue. Second, and most importantly, he knew what was happening was morally wrong. These points are critical to you as a business leader.

On one hand, inaction on your part in confronting volatile employee situations can lead to disaster for your business. Your kingdom vision can fail to materialize if hatred and bitterness are permitted to exist in your organization. God will not allow Himself to be disgraced by a company that is Christian outwardly, but fighting internally.

More importantly, you must be able to recognize injustice from Scripture and do the right thing by undoing it. It doesn't matter if some of the most powerful and important people in your organization are in the wrong. You must address it. Perhaps you fear that confronting them will result in their quitting or not giving a strong effort. Maybe you think they will be demoralized or angry, and intentionally cause your company to lose business. Did those things matter to Nehemiah? Not at all. Just as he had the courage and faith to do the right thing, so should you and I. We have the God of truth and justice on our side. He is greater than any injury that a powerful or important employee can impose upon us. He can overrule any situation, and He is honored when we stand up for what is right without fear.

Turning back to Nehemiah, notice that he addressed the exact injustices that were occurring, and he appealed to their sense of responsibility and allegiance to God. In a sense, what he says is, "The world is watching you and is aware of the wrongs you are committing. Is that really the way Christians should behave? Do you really want them to make fun of you and call you a hypocrite? Shouldn't you really stop doing this and behave as a true Christian"? In other words, he appeals to their faith, the essence of who they are, and the reason they are engaging in this project. He tells them they have lost their distinctiveness and are behaving just like the heathen people.

This is a very strong way to confront your employees in these types of difficult situations. Appealing to the root of their being, the very core of who they are, and making them confront their actions in light of God's Word is the best way to bring someone back on the right track. Hebrews 4:12 says, "For the word of God is living and active, sharper than any two-edged sword, piercing to the division of soul and of spirit, of joints and of marrow, discerning the thoughts and intentions of the heart." This supports the fact that there is no more powerful way to confront someone than by using God's Word.

How did the nobles and wealthy people respond to this confrontation? They admitted their guilt and agreed to the terms set forth by Nehemiah. They said they would return everything they had taken through injustice and would stop lending at usurious rates. In short, they were convicted by Nehemiah's appeal to the lack of congruity between their faith and their treatment of fellow team members.

If your people are truly seeking to exemplify Christ in their lives, they, too, will respond to you when you bring God's Word to their attention. It doesn't have to be in a self-righteous way, but it should be direct and honest. Your people will respect you for handling situations in this way.

As an exclamation point to assure compliance with his requirements, Nehemiah makes the nobles and officials take an oath that is witnessed by the priests. This is the equivalent of our legal agreements. He promises severe consequences for anyone who did not comply with the terms of the oath. We see another side of Nehemiah here. He didn't just allow the nobles and officials to get away with a promise of verbal compliance. Instead, he was tough and shrewd enough to draw up a witnessed legal document that would ensure compliance.

In the same way, you and I want to be trusting and forgiving of our fellow believers. However, the reality of the situation dictates that we protect our businesses and employees by creating written documentation that ensures consequences if offending employees fail to comply with the terms we require from them. The unfortunate truth is that even believers can fail to keep their word. Some people have lifelong habits they simply cannot break, and this practically ensures reoccurrences of problem situations. Of course, you have to be prepared to enforce agreements such as written warnings or probationary terms. Do you have any doubt that Nehemiah would have enforced any of the agreements he made?

An Unselfish Leader: Verses 14-19

The second part of Nehemiah chapter 5 is much more pleasant to deal with and gives us a picture of an unselfish leader. In contrast to the nobles and officials who were using their positions to capitalize on the desperate situations of the poor people in order to enrich themselves, Nehemiah shows us that he actually took less of what was due to him in order to ease the burdens of the people.

Based on the laws at the time, Nehemiah could have lived the high life by demanding money, food, and wine from the people. In addition, he could have had more food and could have acquired property. Other rulers had done these same things in the past, and precedence would lead us to think the people certainly expected it. However, Nehemiah had a different plan. A plan to be distinct. A plan to be an example. A plan to lead in the Spirit of Christ.

Nehemiah said he wanted to be different out of reverence for God. That needs to be the driving force for you and me as kingdom business leaders. If you and I stop revering Christ and putting Him on a pedestal as the guiding light of our business, the entire purpose of the operation is destroyed. Our customers and employees are watching us. Most have seen or heard of business owners or CEOs who are harsh or "greedy." Let's surprise all of them by emulating Nehemiah.

What did he do? As a people developer, he and his men devoted themselves to the work and did not let themselves get distracted by the riches and niceties available to them. They did not allow themselves to become prideful and conceited because of their powerful positions. They were generous to the people, worked with them, and considered their needs. This behavior points us directly to Christ and, in fact, leads us to that incredible passage of Philippians 2:5-11, which says:

> Have this mind among yourselves, which is yours in Christ Jesus, who, though he was in the form of God, did not count equality with God a thing to be grasped, but made himself nothing, taking the form of a servant, being born in the likeness of men. And being found in human form, he humbled himself by becoming obedient to the point of death, even death on a cross. Therefore God has highly exalted him and bestowed on him the name that is above every name, so that at the name of Jesus every knee should bow, in heaven and on earth and under the earth, and every tongue confess that Jesus Christ is Lord, to the glory of God the Father.

The examples of Nehemiah and Jesus show us beyond question what God expects from His leaders. He expects you and me to be generous, focused, empathetic, humble, and hardworking. If Jesus can put aside His position to be humble in order to ensure you and I could come into His kingdom, certainly, it is incumbent upon us to emulate the same type of behavior toward our customers and employees. Remember, we have what we have because of God's grace. He gave us the skills we have to become leaders, and worked out all the circumstances of our lives to lead us to this point of leadership. We did not get these things on our own. Nehemiah recognized this fact and showed us the true way to behave as kingdom leaders.

This chapter ends with Nehemiah's asking God to remember him favorably due to all he did for the Israelites. What are we to make of this? Is Nehemiah being selfish? Is he doing all of this out of selfish ambition in order to gain a greater blessing from God? Do we finally see a flaw in the man we are holding up as a model? I contend the answer to all these questions is emphatically "no." It is not improper to pray for God's blessing upon ourselves, nor is it without precedent in the Bible. The psalmist prays for himself frequently, and Jesus also prays for Himself. In the Lord's Prayer, we are encouraged to ask the Lord to bless us, and Jesus encourages us to ask Him for things in the Gospel of John.

The distinguishing characteristic is revealed to us in the book of James. He tells us, "You do not have, because you do not ask. You ask and do not receive, because you ask wrongly, to spend it on your passions" (James 4:2-3). James points out that the motivation behind our requests for God's blessing determines whether or not we receive what we ask for. In business terms, if we ask God to make us profitable so we can acquire loads of toys and live an opulent lifestyle, that is not the type of leadership God wants from us, nor is it the kind of leadership He will reward. Conversely, if we ask to be profitable or for Him to bless us so His kingdom work can expand and impact an ever-increasing number of people for Christ, that is the type of motivation God seeks from kingdom business leaders.

View From the Trenches

Since Busy Bees opened, we have had numerous opportunities to confront internal strife among our employees. Occasionally, it has seemed like a tidal wave. I never expected this from Christian employees, and even after having been exposed to it on multiple occasions, I still find myself periodically amazed by the rage and bitterness directed from one employee to another. Fortunately, these situations have become fewer and fewer over time, and I attribute this to two things: praying and learning to handle situations in a more Nehemiah-like manner.

At first, I was fairly hesitant to confront employees regarding their behavior, either out of nervousness or fear that they would quit. Initially, we had a few employees we considered indispensable, so we let them get away with more divisive behavior than we should have. My failure to act swiftly and decisively in these situations prolonged the stress of many employees and probably discredited my leadership.

When I did confront people, I used God's Word, but mistakenly assumed that people would fulfill their promises when they agreed orally that they were not complying with God's Word. I had a naive notion that all Christians would be good to their word and everything would be better.

The poor results we realized from following that path have led us to become much more like Nehemiah with our written documentation. Experience and faith have taught us to meet situations just like Nehemiah, directly and honestly, with a full set of written requirements someone must perform in order to regain good standing and keep his job. We finally got to the point where we decided we didn't care how good or popular an employee was, or how much damage we thought she might do in the community if we fired her. We decided that God is God, and He will oversee and protect our actions if we act in faith to do the right thing.

We are now relatively quick to either fire employees or put them on probation, depending on the situation. Since we have followed this approach, we seem to have purged the unproductive employees and retained the good ones. There is less stress among our good employees now, and they are even more productive. The work environment is much warmer and friendlier, and I believe the employees respect my leadership. They know I care about them and am committed to helping them, but they also know that I will take swift action if their actions fall outside the bounds of our core Christian values.

Regarding generosity, we do not have 150 people at our dinner table each day, but we do try to show appreciation to our people through good pay, bonuses, Christmas gifts, and recognition. We try to visit with them often and take an interest in their work as well as their lives. During our team meetings, I emphasize that we are all part of a kingdom team with different roles and responsibilities, and as each employee is reviewing his progress toward his goals, I also let him know the things I am working on for the business.

On the issue of praying to be blessed, I do pray for Busy Bees to be profitable as well as to have a significant kingdom impact on our employees, students, and parents. During the days when we were losing money by the bucketful, I do confess that my prayers were much more oriented toward profitability than toward having a kingdom impact. The stress of having so much financial pressure took my mind in that direction frequently.

In addition, it is easy for my mind to wander and think solely about the vast amount of money a business such as ours is capable of producing. I find that I have to consciously turn those thoughts off and focus on asking God to bless our efforts to have a kingdom influence. I know we have to be wise concerning the money; otherwise, we can quickly go broke. However, that is not our consuming thought. It really never has been, but it is easy to start thinking about the new boat or furniture the business can buy for us instead of maintaining focus on delivering the message of Christ to small children and their families.

I find that it is a continual progression of praying and training my mind to focus simultaneously on good business, people, and Christian principles, trust in God more and more to use His power to build the business. There is a sense in which I believe God enables our businesses to prosper financially according to the rate at which we are capable of responsibly handling money. I know this is not a hard and fast rule, but it does seem from the passage in the book of James referenced earlier that God blesses us more as our motivations conform more and more to His will.

Chapter 9

The Leader Is Targeted for Destruction: Nehemiah Chapter 6

You will be hated by all for my name's sake. But the one who endures to the end will be saved.

Matthew 10:22

In the last two chapters, we have seen God's enemies try to disrupt the work on the wall. First they tried direct intimidation and threats against the people, trying to get them to stop the rebuilding of the wall out of fear. After that failed, they tried another tactic, creating dissension among the kingdom team members in order to destroy the team from within. In this chapter, Nehemiah tells us about a third tactic of the enemy. This time they use direct threats and deception against Nehemiah in order to either discredit his leadership among the people, do physical harm to him, or both. Nehemiah shows us just how important it is for a leader to have a solid faith in God and the vision He has given him. If Nehemiah had not possessed those characteristics, he could easily have been defeated by a very tenacious enemy. However, because he did not give in, but instead stood fast for God, generations of people came to know the Lord.

What about you? Will you stand fast in the face of great personal adversity? What are the consequences for future generations if you let yourself be intimidated or discouraged so that you decide pursuing what God has laid on your heart is not worth the trouble? We will explore these questions and more in this chapter.

[1]Now when Sanballat and Tobiah and Geshem the Arab and the rest of our enemies heard that I had built the wall and that there was no breach left in it (although up to that time I had not set up the doors in the gates), [2]Sanballat and Geshem sent to me, saying, "Come and let us meet together at Hakkephirim in the plain of Ono." But they intended to do me harm. [3]And I sent messengers to them, saying, "I am doing a great work and I cannot come down. Why should the work stop while I leave it and come down to you?" [4]And they sent to me four times in this way, and I answered them in the same manner. [5]In the same way Sanballat for the fifth time sent his servant to me with an open letter in his hand. [6]In it was written, "It is reported among the nations, and Geshem also says it, that you and the Jews intend to rebel; that is why you are building the wall. And according to these reports you wish to become their king. [7]And you have also set up prophets to proclaim concerning you in Jerusalem, 'There is a king in Judah.' And now the king will hear of these reports. So now come and let us take counsel together." [8]Then I sent to him, saying, "No such things as you say have been done, for you are inventing them out of your own mind." [9]For they all wanted to frighten us, thinking, "Their hands will drop from the work, and it will not be done." But now, O God, strengthen my hands.

[10]Now when I went into the house of Shemaiah the son of Delaiah, son of Mehetabel, who was confined to his home, he said, "Let us meet together in the house of God, within the temple. Let us close the doors of the temple, for they are coming to kill you. They are coming to kill you by night." [11]But I said, "Should such a man as I run away? And what man such as I could go into the temple and live? I will not go in." [12]And I understood and saw that God had not sent him, but he had pronounced the prophecy against me because Tobiah and Sanballat had hired him. [13]For this purpose he

was hired, that I should be afraid and act in this way and sin, and so they could give me a bad name in order to taunt me. [14]Remember Tobiah and Sanballat, O my God, according to these things that they did, and also the prophetess Noadiah and the rest of the prophets who wanted to make me afraid.

[15]So the wall was finished on the twenty-fifth day of the month Elul, in fifty-two days. [16]And when all our enemies heard of it, all the nations around us were afraid and fell greatly in their own esteem, for they perceived that this work had been accomplished with the help of our God. [17]Moreover, in those days the nobles of Judah sent many letters to Tobiah, and Tobiah's letters came to them. [18]For many in Judah were bound by oath to him, because he was the son-in-law of Shecaniah the son of Arah: and his son Jehohanan had taken the daughter of Meshullam the son of Berechiah as his wife. [19]Also they spoke of his good deeds in my presence and reported my words to him. And Tobiah sent letters to make me afraid.

Just imagine how desperate Sanballat, Tobiah, and Geshem must have felt as they saw the wall completely built with no gaps in it. They had to have known that life as they knew it was over. The Jews were going to rebuild their culture and reestablish their faith and worship of God. Moreover, these three men, no doubt, stood to lose considerable influence, power, or wealth as a result of the Jews being strengthened and revitalized.

This gives us a picture of Christianity today. Jesus Christ has filled the gaps in the wall, and the enemy knows life as he knows it is over. He is defeated, yet he still fights on. Nevertheless, we know Jesus has secured the victory for us. Romans 8:37 tells us, "We are more than conquerors through him who loved us." However, there are still difficult battles to be fought, so let's see how we can prepare ourselves for the tough fights.

Visualize your business for a minute. You have worked hard to establish a new product line that is really necessary in order for your kingdom business to succeed. You and your team have worked hard and have overcome many obstacles to get to this point. Now ask yourself this question: "Who stands to lose if I win?" Maybe it's a competitor in your town, or even overseas. Perhaps it is a disgruntled government official who had a bad religious experience as a child and is opposed to all things Christian. Maybe it is the enemy in your mind that is creating fear and hesitation. Whatever, wherever, or whoever your enemy is, know that a strong and threatened foe will stop at nothing to try to tear you down personally so your kingdom business fails.

After making several unsuccessful attempts to intimidate your workers or make untrue accusations about your company in the marketplace, maybe your fierce competitor decides he needs to come after you personally as he sees that your company's success is inevitable. That's exactly what happened to Nehemiah.

Up to this point, the Jews had withstood verbal assaults and threats of violence as well as an internal scandal. Despite all that adversity, they had nearly completed this project through God's protection and the prayerful and courageous leadership of Nehemiah. Desperate, his enemies tried to lure him into several traps, finally resorting to lies, extortion, and even using people within the Jewish community to discredit and destabilize Nehemiah's leadership.

First, his enemies tried to distract him by luring him away from the project. Nehemiah doesn't elaborate, but maybe they had promised him some kind of lucrative partnership. Second, they made false accusations against him and threatened to report him to the king. Third, they tried to deceive him into hiding in fear.

In all these threats, we see some stellar qualities in Nehemiah, which we should try to emulate. He continually shows great discernment and focus on his goal, which enables him to see through all the threats, intimidation, and deception. Nehemiah realized how vital it was to maintain integrity in his role. The completion of the project hinged on his focused, courageous, and consistent leadership. If he had negotiated with the enemies, believed their deception, or fled in fear, the people would have been demoralized and the work may very well have stopped.

Characteristically, we see Nehemiah going to prayer for strength. Imagine how stressful this must have been for him. He had left a comfortable position working in the king's court in exchange for working in a dusty desert with an impoverished and weak labor force, and enemies inside and outside trying to ensure his defeat. What kept him going? Purely and simply, his relationship with God and his sense of knowing what God had called him to do. He had his mind focused on what God wanted him to do and would stop at nothing until he had accomplished his mission.

What was the result of Nehemiah's steadfastness? The wall was built in fifty-two days, and God was glorified in the eyes of the surrounding enemy nations. According to the best guesses of archaeologists, the wall covered an irregularly shaped area somewhere between 1.5 and 2.5 miles around its perimeter. Imagine building that wall by hand from pieces of rubble in fifty-two days. To me, that seems incredibly fast, and it could only have been done with a great plan and focused team and leader. In addition, it made such an impact on the other nations that they realized God was truly in the midst of the Israelites.

As a Christian business leader, you can expect to come under attack personally, especially if you and your team are successful. Why would the enemy want to attack an unsuccessful team? What threat would it be to him?

When you are attacked, will you be prepared? Are you working on your relationship with God on a regular basis through prayer, study of His Word, worship, and fellowship? Do you have a good sense of discernment regarding people's motives and what they are telling you? I know I am lied to all the time, but it is not always easy to know the difference between complete fact, complete fiction, or a combination. Sometimes there are different versions of the truth, depending on the perspectives of different people. It takes prayer and wisdom to know what to believe.

Through all the adversity, the only thing you can truly rely on is to stay focused on your internal beacon, that sense of calling God has placed in your heart for your business. It is easy to get distracted by well-meaning people, but it is even more upsetting to be attacked by people who, for whatever reason, dislike you and want you to fail. Stay true to your mission. Follow Nehemiah's example, and see the results God can accomplish through you as well as the impact you and your kingdom team have on "the surrounding nations."

View From the Trenches

The last thing I expected in operating a Christian preschool was to be personally attacked for anything. I was shocked when those things began to happen. Of course, that was before I read Nehemiah and really started thinking about the trials of Jesus, Paul, Joseph, and a host of other biblical figures.

We have been sued, cursed, slandered, told we were the reason people didn't want to come to Christ, and accused of being sick and demented for making money off of the name of Christ. None of these were pleasant, and all created a great deal of stress in our household and business. Throughout all of these different attacks, God has enabled me to be calm and focused even when I wanted to be enraged. I always know my team, customers, and suppliers are evaluating my reactions in light of being a Christian, so I pray for strength and try to keep myself and my team focused on spreading the gospel to little children and their families.

Sometimes these attacks do take time to address. We have had to go to court and defend ourselves on several occasions, and that has wasted our time as well as that of our staff. Even with allocating some time and energy to adverse situations such as these, it has been so important for me to help my team stay focused on the main thing. Without my leadership, it would be easy for them to become embroiled in the inflammatory circumstances, but we simply cannot devote excessive time to these issues.

In the first two years, we seemed to get more distracted on these difficult issues, and valuable time was wasted that we could have spent marketing, selling, or developing joint relationships with businesses serving our same market. Now, in our third year, we appear to have become more disciplined and focused, and those have come from having a more seasoned staff as well as from my becoming more experienced.

One thing that can result from these personal attacks is discouragement. For me, there have been many times when I thought how nice my life would be if I just gave up Busy Bees. Even now, when our enrollment is stabilized and we are making a profit, there are times when I yearn for a simple life and sometimes wonder if we did the right thing by starting Busy Bees. Maybe Nehemiah also yearned for his days as a cupbearer during the times when he was personally attacked with great intensity.

What really keeps me going when we hit these rough spots is my sense of God's calling. Just like Nehemiah, I try to reflect back on the vision God gave us, the doors He opened for us, and the distance He has allowed us to travel. I also think about the lives we have influenced and the compliments we have received, and that helps me regain my sense of commitment and confidence that we're doing the right thing. Not long ago, I walked into a Busy Bees classroom near closing time, and a child was reciting for his mother the Bible verse he had learned. Scenes like that make everything worthwhile.

I'm sure you sometimes get discouraged, too. You might even feel like giving up. I'll say it again: You need to remember your calling. Yes, sometimes it is appropriate to throw in the towel and close your business. We don't need to go broke for the Lord. But don't let the fact that things are hard discourage you. Nowhere in the Bible does it say building God's kingdom will be easy. God's own Son had to die to save us, and Joshua had to battle all his life, so why should you or I expect things to be easy? Remember Nehemiah's example. Stay focused on your calling and the vision God gave you, no matter who tries to disrupt your business.

Another element we see from Nehemiah chapter 6 is the principle of being very careful whom you listen to. While Nehemiah was being deceived by enemies, sometimes our well-meaning friends, family members, and employees give us well-meaning, but poor, advice. Consider the fact that these folks probably never had the same vision for your business that God has placed on your heart, so their advice can come from a different perspective than what you might have.

For example, most do not have an entrepreneurial background, so their risk tolerance may be lower than yours. I try to listen to other people for their particular expertise, such as accounting and finance, state regulations pertaining to our business, and nutritional needs of children. When I understand their technical perspective, I then take it into consideration as part of the overall strategy of Busy Bees. What I'm saying is you have to reserve the strategic decisions for yourself. You can receive input, but you need to own the strategy so you can be true to God's calling on you and your kingdom business. If you start delegating strategy to people who are not entrepreneurs and who haven't received your call, I believe your business will lose focus and struggle to fulfill its mission.

In the face of adversity, remember the words of the apostle Paul in Philippians chapter 1: "I am sure of this, that he who began a good work in you will bring it to completion at the day of Jesus Christ."

Chapter 10

Filling Key Leadership Positions: Nehemiah 7:1-3

Moses' father-in-law said to him, "What you are doing is not good. You and the people with you will certainly wear yourselves out, for the thing is too heavy for you. You are not able to do it alone.

Exodus 18:17-18

Moreover, look for able men from all the people, men who fear God, who are trustworthy and hate a bribe, and place such men over the people as chiefs of thousands, of hundreds, of fifties, and of tens. And let them judge the people at all times. Every great matter they shall bring to you, but any small matter they shall decide themselves. So it will be easier for you, and they will bear the burden with you. If you do this, God will direct you, you will be able to endure, and all this people also will go to their place in peace.

Exodus 18:21-23

Chapter 7 of Nehemiah contains three critical pieces of insight for your kingdom business, so please give these your undivided attention. The first element comes from the first three verses, and the topic is leadership selection and direction. The second element goes from verse 4 to 69 and involves recordkeeping, analysis, and knowledge of your customers. The third section shows us that God acknowledges the work of each of His kingdom soldiers, from the greatest to the least. Let's take these one at a time beginning with leadership selection and direction.

> [1]Now when the wall had been built and I had set up the doors, and the gatekeepers, the singers, and the Levites had been appointed, [2]I gave my brother Hanani and Hananiah the governor of the castle charge over Jerusalem, for he was a more faithful and God-fearing man than many. [3]And I said to them, "Let not the gates of Jerusalem be opened until the sun is hot. And while they are still standing guard, let them shut and bar the doors. Appoint guards from among the inhabitants of Jerusalem, some at their guard posts and some in front of their own homes."

Leadership Selection and Direction

After the wall was completed, the first thing Nehemiah did was appoint people to perform the various functions needed to keep the city going. This included appointing Hanani and Hananiah to the highest leadership positions. We see one characteristic of Hananiah, that he feared God more than most. In addition, Nehemiah left these two men with simple, but important, instructions. Besides those, he did not spell out every detail of their jobs for them.

Why is it that so many businesses fail, and those who do make it frequently have burned-out owners? According to Michael Gerber, author of *The E-Myth Revisited* and many other good books on small business, the primary reason for burnout is so many business owners are "doing it, doing it, doing it." What he means is that they are "working in their business" on the small details instead of "working on their business," meaning creating the systems, direction, and big picture. According to Gerber, many business owners trade their corporate jobs for a job in their own business, and consequently, the business never grows because the owner never learns how to choose and train right leaders to manage the business.

If your kingdom business is to grow into a powerful force for God's kingdom, you are going to have to learn to let go of various parts of it and give those parts to other people. This is not a news flash, but it is something frequently neglected by business owners. Besides developing your vision and providing direction for your company, this is by far your most important task. Since you are finite in your time, resources, and abilities, the growth of your company is dependent upon your finding, motivating, and training other leaders who share your same vision and are passionate about carrying it out.

I hear you complaining right now. "Nobody can do things as well as I can. It is hard to find people with a strong work ethic that I can trust. Every time I finally get someone trained, he quits." And on and on. Let's just think about that for a minute or two. I seem to recall that the Creator of the universe came down from heaven to become a baby, and then grow into a man. As His ministry began, He selected twelve guys to be His direct reports. He spent about three years teaching them, and he gave them the most important job that any supervisor has ever given a direct report. But wait, these men were not all highly educated or well-known socially. They were average men of the day without impressive resumes, degrees from prominent schools, or even experience in the field into which He called them. Yet He called them nevertheless. His training program was pretty impressive, too. Only one of them went to the other side. The rest remained with the team, and their work has influenced the history of the world.

I hope you get the point of this little tangent. If Jesus could choose ordinary men to do the monumental work of spreading the gospel and building the early church, surely, you can find some leaders to help you with your company. No, it won't be pleasant. Yes, it will be painful. I have no doubt that you will go through several people at least before you lock onto the right person or people. That's just the way it is. Accept it and work with it. Read books or take classes on leadership training. I highly recommend the works of John Maxwell. In the long run, it will be worth it to you to be freed up to work on the most important elements of your company instead of having to be involved in every decision and task.

If you are a veteran manager or leader, you know what I am talking about. This skill of choosing and training the right leaders, and giving them the proper focus, is difficult to master, and is sorely lacking in today's business world. Basically, it is discipling, which is what Jesus did with the twelve apostles. We will discuss the topic of discipling more in Nehemiah chapter 8, but for now, be thinking about what tasks would be better performed by people other than you, and who you can be discipling to take on those roles. The leaders you choose won't be perfect, but neither are you. Neither were Jesus' picks. This is part of the people development process we began discussing in chapter 3, and as a people developer, there is no more important task for you to perform than choosing leaders who can help develop other people.

Returning to Nehemiah, remember, we saw that he focused his two main leaders on two important tasks, but did not give them much detail concerning the rest of their jobs. Maybe Nehemiah left out the details intentionally, but I suspect he did not try to micromanage them. Instead, he backed off and gave them space to do their jobs.

Likewise, you need to understand what the most important tasks are for your leaders to accomplish, but you also have to trust them enough to do their jobs. It's like what Ronald Reagan used to say about the Soviet Union: "Trust, but verify." Make sure your leaders know what the most important priorities are, give them some examples and ideas of how to do those tasks if they need concrete examples, and measure their progress. If you are too hands-off and don't give them sufficient focus, they will find their own focus, but it might not be on the things most important to you. Typically, they will slide into busy operational-type work instead of focusing on increasing profitability, improving product quality, creating better customer service, or getting and keeping more customers. That's why you will need to continually train, coach, and measure. As your efforts begin to bear fruit, and your leaders develop and become more trustworthy in terms of their level of skill and commitment to your vision, you will be surprised at the level of creativity and innovation they show you.

The big point here is that you will have to identify the most important tasks and make sure they get done by using clear communication as well as measurement. Using the 80/20 principle mentioned earlier to help you identify and focus on the most important things can accelerate the progress of your business faster than you can imagine.

View From the Trenches

If you remember from the introduction, Cindy homeschools our children, and I have a full-time job at the bank. Neither Cindy nor I have ever worked one minute at the school with any regularly assigned duties. Instead, we designed our business from the beginning, knowing how important this idea of choosing and training leaders would be.

Yes, this has been difficult, but it is paying off. Busy Bees has two leaders: a chief operating officer and a director. My mother, Cindy McClymonds Sr., has done a remarkable job as COO, and our current director is performing well. The two of them handle budgeting, hiring and firing, day-to-day management of the teachers, customer service, and every other aspect of the school. While Cindy and I are drinking coffee early in the morning, our leaders are running the school. When Cindy is teaching Andrew and Emmy, other people are running Busy Bees for us. When I am working with my employees at the bank, other folks are spreading the gospel and making money for us.

We do not micromanage our leaders or employees. We have tried to create rigorous hiring standards, even to the point of testing. In addition, in all our dealings and meetings with employees, we try to communicate the vision of the school and underscore the missionary aspect of their jobs. If we do these things right, we believe our leaders and employees will have an important sense of personal worth and vision, and will do their best for Busy Bees. So far, this has worked out well for us.

Cindy and I focus our energies on making the most difficult personnel decisions, setting marketing and sales strategy, encouraging innovation, training our leaders, and making sure our employees know we care about them. I take one lunch hour per week to meet with our director, spend two hours per month going to lunch with employees, and spend one hour per month in a team meeting. Other than that, our work in the evenings focuses on marketing, communicating via email with our leaders, and examining reports and numbers, which we will discuss in the next part of Nehemiah chapter 7.

It is true that being able to work in our business may have allowed the school to progress more rapidly, but here we are just under three years into our existence, and we have been profitable over the last seven months. By God's grace and a lot of hard work, things have turned around remarkably.

This has not been an easy task, but our situation dictated that we learn to hand the reins over to other people that God brought to us. I am almost embarrassed to admit that we have had five directors in the almost three years we have been open. Two were let go, and the other two would have been if they hadn't quit first. It would not do you justice if I were to gloss over our great frustration with having this many directors. It has made us question our management and leadership practices. Early on, we definitely gave each director too much freedom. Now we have corrected much of that through greater emphasis on management reporting as well as more purposeful meetings.

Staying in touch with the teachers and other non-management employees has been most helpful in evaluating our directors. In addition to their appreciating my taking an interest in them, they are not shy about telling me the truth about those in management above them. If I hear a consistent theme running through each employee meeting, I know I have enough evidence to put further pressure on the director. One director was let go as a direct result of having these employee meetings. I suspected she was not pulling her weight and was bringing down morale. At our meetings, however, she seemed positive and upbeat. It was all window dressing for the boss.

Trying to find directors that have management experience, good judgment, a strong work ethic, and a commitment to Christ has been tremendously difficult, to say the least. Most have had at least a modest commitment to Christ, but few have had management experience, good judgment, or a sound work ethic. In spite of the failings of these leaders, and our corresponding failure in hiring them, God has been so faithful to us. He has blessed us with good teachers and has continued to allow the school to grow and build a solid reputation. Just as God used flawed human leaders throughout the ages to bring about His kingdom, He has used the flawed owners and directors of Busy Bees to build a school that brings glory to Him.

These difficulties did not tempt us to begin working day to day at the school. They were hard and stressful to deal with, but through prayer and encouragement from His Word, they gave us strength and wisdom to persevere.

Our current director is doing a fine job. Is she perfect? Does she do everything the way I want her to do it? No to both. However, we are imperfect owners as well. Despite some differences we have, her work ethic is strong, her judgment is improving, she is willing to learn, and she is actively growing in her faith. The teachers and parents respect and trust her, which is invaluable. What's the difference between now and the past?

I think it has been a learning experience to ensure we communicate effectively and measure expectations, and hold them accountable. We are also no longer afraid to fire poor performers. It sounds easy, and I always thought we were doing that. However, with each failed manager, we have worked all the more diligently to make sure the next director truly understands what we want and is able and willing to carry it out. Our current director is a graduate of the six-week leadership development program I also conducted, so she is fully versed in the background and philosophy of the school.

Please do not overlook this aspect of your business. Study the 80/20 principle. Spend time analyzing what the most important tasks are for you as well as for the leaders you hire. Take time to train them and help them understand your vision for the company. Let them know how their actions on a daily basis fit into the big picture. Give them some latitude to develop their own personality and management style. They are not you, and they are not going to do things exactly as you would. As long as the result is acceptable, that's okay. Get over it. Back them up in front of your other employees, and let them know you are behind them. Don't be surprised if you have to work your way through several leaders before finally finding one who is satisfactory. Pray continually that God would bring people to you that you can help disciple as leaders. Remember that your main business is the people development business.

Chapter 11

The Importance of Numbers: Nehemiah 7:4-69

Are not two sparrows sold for a penny? And not one of them will fall to the ground apart from your Father. But even the hairs of your head are all numbered. Fear not, therefore; you are of more value than many sparrows.

Matthew 10:29-31

How many of you really enjoy accounting, getting up to your elbows in the numbers, analyzing revenue and expenses, looking at financial ratios? How about looking at marketing and sales data to spot trends? Sounds like fun, right? Do you know each and every customer by name, and is the service you deliver to them tailored to their individual needs, or is your business "one size fits all"?

If you are like many business entrepreneurs, the thought of setting up systems for finance and accounting, marketing, and customer service is not very appealing to you. The prospect of analyzing data is even less appealing and seems more like having a tooth pulled without Novocain. Many of us would rather work on the "big picture" and leave these details to subordinates or outsourced partners. Maybe you are not very good at recordkeeping accounting or bookkeeping. You would rather create, sell, and build your business. Many of us prefer to leave the numbers to someone else.

Well, fortunately for us, God is a good recordkeeper. He keeps a close eye on His numbers, and He delivers individual service to each of His chosen people. In addition, He takes careful note of the work His people do for the kingdom. As we explore this long list of names encountered in chapter 7, we will see how our loving God keeps track of His people, and we will make application to our businesses. This section contains a focus on numbers as well as on relationships, so there should be something here for you, whether you are analytical or relational in nature, or both. Let's read verses 4 through 73 now.

⁴The city was wide and large, but the people within it were few, and no houses had been rebuilt.

⁵Then my God put it into my heart to assemble the nobles and the officials and the people to be enrolled by genealogy. And I found the book of the genealogy of those who came up at the first, and I found written in it:

⁶These were the people of the province who came up out of the captivity of those exiles whom Nebuchadnezzar the king of Babylon had carried into exile. They returned to Jerusalem and Judah, each to his town. ⁷They came with Zerubbabel, Jeshua, Nehemiah, Azariah, Raamiah, Nahamani, Mordecai, Bilshan, Mispereth, Bigvai, Nehum, Baanah.

The number of the men of the people of Israel: ⁸the sons of Parosh, 2,172. ⁹The sons of Shephatiah, 372. ¹⁰The sons of Arah, 652. ¹¹The sons of Pahath-moab, namely the sons of Jeshua and Joab, 2,818. ¹²The sons of Elam, 1,254. ¹³The sons of Zattu, 845. ¹⁴The sons of Zaccai, 760. ¹⁵The sons of Binnui, 648. ¹⁶The sons of Bebai, 628. ¹⁷The sons of Azgad, 2,322. ¹⁸The sons of Adonikam, 667. ¹⁹The sons of Bigvai, 2,067. ²⁰The sons of Adin, 655. ²¹The sons of Ater, namely of Hezekiah, 98. ²²The sons of Hashum, 328. ²³The sons of Bezai, 324. ²⁴The sons of Hariph, 112. ²⁵The sons of Gibeon, 95. ²⁶The men of Bethlehem and Netophah, 188. ²⁷The men of Anathoth, 128. ²⁸The men of Beth-azmaveth, 42. ²⁹The men of Kiriath-jearim, Chephirah, and Beeroth, 743. ³⁰The men of Ramah and Geba, 621. ³¹The men of Michmas, 122.

³²The men of Bethel and Ai, 123. ³³The men of the other Nebo, 52. ³⁴The sons of the other Elam, 1,254. ³⁵The sons of Harim, 320. ³⁶The sons of Jericho, 345. ³⁷The sons of Lod, Hadid, and Ono, 721. ³⁸The sons of Senaah, 3,930.

³⁹The priests: the sons of Jedaiah, namely the house of Jeshua, 973. ⁴⁰The sons of Immer, 1,052. ⁴¹The sons of Pashhur, 1,247. ⁴²The sons of Harim, 1,017.

⁴³The Levites: the sons of Jeshua, namely of Kadmiel of the sons of Hodevah, 74. ⁴⁴The singers: the sons of Asaph, 148. ⁴⁵The gatekeepers: the sons of Shallum, the sons of Ater, the sons of Talmon, the sons of Akkub, the sons of Hatita, the sons of Shobai, 138.

⁴⁶The temple servants: the sons of Ziha, the sons of Hasupha, the sons of Tabbaoth, ⁴⁷the sons of Keros, the sons of Sia, the sons of Padon, ⁴⁸the sons of Lebana, the sons of Hagaba, the sons of Shalmai, ⁴⁹the sons of Hanan, the sons of Giddel, the sons of Gahar, ⁵⁰the sons of Reaiah, the sons of Rezin, the sons of Nekoda, ⁵¹the sons of Gazzam, the sons of Uzza, the sons of Paseah, ⁵²the sons of Besai, the sons of Meunim, the sons of Nephushesim, ⁵³the sons of Bakbuk, the sons of Hakupha, the sons of Harhur, ⁵⁴the sons of Bazlith, the sons of Mehida, the sons of Harsha, ⁵⁵the sons of Barkos, the sons of Sisera, the sons of Temah, ⁵⁶the sons of Neziah, the sons of Hatipha.

⁵⁷The sons of Solomon's servants: the sons of Sotai, the sons of Sophereth, the sons of Perida, ⁵⁸the sons of Jaala, the sons of Darkon, the sons of Giddel, ⁵⁹the sons of Shephatiah, the sons of Hattil, the sons of Pochereth-hazzebaim, the sons of Amon.

⁶⁰All the temple servants and the sons of Solomon's servants were 392.

⁶¹The following were those who came up from Tel-melah, Tel-harsha, Cherub, Addon, and Immer, but they could not prove their fathers' houses nor their descent, whether they belonged to Israel: ⁶²the sons of Delaiah, the sons of Tobiah, the sons of Nekoda, 642. ⁶³Also, of the priests: the sons of Hobaiah, the sons of Hakkoz, the sons of Barzillai (who had

taken a wife of the daughters of Barzillai the Gileadite and was called by their name). [64]These sought their registration among those enrolled in the genealogies, but it was not found there, so they were excluded from the priesthood as unclean. [65]The governor told them that they were not to partake of the most holy food until a priest with Urim and Thummim should arise.

[66]The whole assembly together was 42,360, [67]besides their male and female servants, of whom there were 7,337. And they had 245 singers, male and female. [68]Their horses were 736, their mules 245, [69]their camels 435, and their donkeys 6,720.

To this point, Nehemiah had completed the first main objective of his vision of restoring the Jews to a strong, God-fearing society. He had rebuilt the wall, but the houses were not yet rebuilt, and few people lived in the city. The next phase of his plan was to get people living in the city. After all, why go to all the trouble of rebuilding the walls if no one was going to live in Jerusalem?

To determine who was eligible to live in the city, Nehemiah had to be able to distinguish from a legal standpoint between those who were Jews and those who were not. In order to do this, God put it on Nehemiah's heart to compare the families living in the region with a genealogical record of the Jews who had returned from Babylon with Ezra years earlier.

In these verses, we see a long list of families with differing occupations and social status. There are priests, servants, singers, common people, and everything in between. This long list does not contain just the names of families; it also shows us the number of people within each family. In verses 66 through 69, Nehemiah sums up all the totals for us, including the numbers of horses, mules, camels, and donkeys.

While this is a book on business and not theology, I have to let you know that this list has great theological importance. You will see that it applies to your business because it is the remarkable fulfillment of one of God's promises. By application, if we see God keeping His merciful promise of redemption to people who were unfaithful to Him, why would He not in the same manner keep His promises to you? To see exactly what I mean, read 2 Chronicles 36:15-23. These verses paint a very sad story of the fall of Jerusalem, the destruction of the city's walls, and the murdering of some of its inhabitants as well as the remaining ones being taken into captivity. In the same passage, however, we read that Jeremiah's prophesy of Israel being released from captivity after seventy years came true through the decree of the pagan King Cyrus. So we see destruction and the fulfillment of a promise of redemption all in one passage. How does this apply to the list of names here in Nehemiah chapter 7? These names are the people who were actually released from captivity after seventy years. They are the fulfillment of God's promise of redemption.

Taking it a step further, these families represent the covenant God made to Abraham, that his descendants would be as numerous as the stars and the sand on the seashore. This passage shows us that God's covenants and the building of His kingdom are carried out through families. These family names show us the importance that God places on families. We will study this further in Nehemiah chapter 10, but it is important to bring it up here.

As we continue to examine this passage, we also note that God knows His people by name. He knows you, me, and our families not only by name, but also by how many there are of us. We are not anonymous to Him. He calls us by name, and just as He has listed the families of His people here in this chapter, so He also has listed the names of His redeemed people in His Book of Life. Remember that God knows you and your family better than even you do. Matthew says He knows us in such detail that even the number of hairs on our head is known to Him.

One more note on this list is that it is symbolic of the redemptive work of Jesus Christ, which was promised as far back as Genesis 3. When Israel fell to the Babylonians because they turned their collective back on God, God judged them as guilty and had them punished. Yet in His great mercy, He chose to restore them, just as He now brings people to restored fellowship with Him through the powerful redeeming work of Jesus Christ. Both Romans 5 and Ephesians 2 tell us we were God's enemies before He brought us to salvation, just as the Jews were who turned their backs on God. Despite this, God showed His love for these people by bringing them back, not because they deserved or earned it, but rather because God is rich in mercy. Likewise, we did not deserve or earn salvation in Christ. God reached out to us while we were still sinners and brought us into His kingdom.

Toward the end of the chapter, we see God not only knows individuals and families, but the entire nation as well. He knows our individual members, and He knows us as the church universal. We are precious to Him individually and collectively. He is not a distant, dispassionate, and disinterested God. No, He is on the move and working through you, me, our families, our churches, and our businesses.

Now that I have given you a mini lesson on the theology of this section, let's examine how to apply it to your business. Since God sets the example for us by keeping good records, we are called as business owners to the same standard. In the following section, we will discuss the topic of quantitative analysis and speak specifically about systems for finance and accounting, marketing, and customer service. One note before we get started is that by a "system," I do not mean only computers or software. Rather, I am referring to establishing good processes, in which software plays an integral role.

Quantitative Analysis

Over the last twenty years in business as a bank employee as well as an entrepreneur, I have encountered many people who are afraid of numbers. They would rather work with and serve people, and they see numbers as just a mundane necessity used to keep score and let them know when they are underperforming.

I hope this is not your opinion. My attitude has always been that numbers are nothing more than puzzle pieces that help business people weave together important stories. That word "story" is key because that is the only thing you want to know. You want to know the story so you can decide what to do next.

For many years, I have taught line managers at banks how to interpret marketing numbers to help fine-tune their marketing strategies and tactics. Unfortunately, the majority of managers would rather forego incorporating numeric analysis into their repertoire of business tools, hoping they can remain competitive by doing the same things they have always done. The few managers who have made diligent efforts to employ the quantitatively based sales and marketing systems my team and I have developed have seen their results skyrocket.

Without a good understanding of numbers, many business efforts result in poor performance because the wrong prospects or customers are targeted with the wrong product offers. On the finance and accounting side, many businesses have phenomenal sales growth, but are unprofitable because the leaders do not sufficiently understand their numbers relating to expenses, accounts receivables, and delinquencies. Moreover, many businesses fail to establish systems of dual control in their finance and accounting systems, leaving the collection and accounting of money to the same people. I won't belabor this point except to say that in both the corporate and small business worlds in which I live, I see a great weakness among many managers and business owners in their ability to understand the numbers of their business. Let's look at some of the key types of numbers every one of us needs to study on an ongoing basis.

Accounting and Finance

I once heard author, speaker, and Coach Bryan Tracy say that while entrepreneurs tend to pay a great deal of attention to product development and operations, the real weakness that destroys businesses is in the area of finance and accounting. Perhaps you are not the accounting type and do not spend much time with your income statement and balance sheet. Maybe you have lax or lenient payment policies and, as a result, have high delinquencies or accounts receivables. If you do not examine your income statement on a regular basis, you may be headed for disaster. If you do not have a budget that you adhere to strictly, your time in business will certainly be short-lived. If you are not trying hard to understand the stories behind your numbers so you can determine which expenses to reduce, which suppliers to fire, and whether or not to raise prices, you may soon find yourself broke. If you are relying on only one employee to keep track of your money, delinquencies, and accounts receivables, you are asking for serious trouble.

I am not an accountant or finance person, so the lesson I deliver to you on this topic will be short and to the point. Point number one is to use some type of accounting software. I assume you are doing this. If not, you need to buy a package today.

Building on that is developing the ability to understand your financial statements. In all my years working in banking in a staff function, I never really had to study income statements and balance sheets from the viewpoint of a business owner. Becoming an entrepreneur suddenly makes your financial statements take on a very personal meaning. They tell you how *your* money is being spent and how much *you* are earning. While it is beyond the scope of this book to tell you how to read these statements, I am going to admonish you that this is a critical part of your responsibility as a kingdom steward. God has entrusted you with a certain amount of wealth, capital, and profits. Just like the parable of the talents taught by Jesus, God has given you these resources to make a profit for His kingdom. Understanding your financial statements and learning to analyze them systematically is an essential part of your achieving the type of excellence as a steward that God desires.

In addition, setting up a system of financial checks and balances between you and other team members is necessary for your financial preservation. By no means am I an expert on setting up these systems, so I suggest you find an accountant or bookkeeper with expertise in this area. A small piece of advice I do have is this: You do not want to put yourself in the position of depending on one person to do this. That person may love you today and hate you tomorrow, and the results probably will not be good for your business. It creates unnecessary risk for the business and creates potential temptation for that one employee.

The other piece of advice I have is to watch your numbers daily and weekly, and ask a lot of questions. Hold people accountable, and don't be afraid to put them on the "hot seat." The more frequently you ask questions, the more informed you will be regarding some of the important nuances in your business. In addition, the more knowledgeable you become in this area, the more likely you will be to be able to discover mistakes, discrepancies, or fraud. You simply have to be highly involved in this aspect of your business. I am not saying you have to be the chief financial officer or book-keeper, but you must develop expertise in this area so you can lead. For further study, I recommend Michael Gerber's book *E-Myth Mastery* or Robert Kiyosaki's book *Before You Quit Your Job*. Both of these provide good guidance for learning to lead your company financially.

Marketing Systems

In contrast to finance and accounting, putting together marketing systems is something I actually know something about because I have been doing it for large corporations for more than twenty years. Transferring this acquired knowledge and experience to a small business with far fewer resources has been challenging, and we will cover that part in "View From the Trenches." In this section, I will briefly attempt to give an overview of the subject, and if you desire more information, you can contact me directly.

The goal of a sales and marketing system, as my team and I define it, is to transform raw data into information that can be used to form strategy and tactics to improve the performance of the business, provide greater service to customers, and bring more success and enjoyment to the employees. As you might guess, this requires a deep understanding of the goals of the business as well as the needs of customers and employees. The skills involved are database management, information analysis, report development, and an excellent ability to put the pieces together into effective sales and marketing activities.

At its simplest level, it involves dividing customers into segments to determine which are the most profitable, how much they buy, what they buy, and why they buy it. You are not attempting to determine the individual needs of unique customers at this point. Rather, you are trying to identify groups of people that are drawn to your service. Then you want to identify the characteristics of those groups of people so you can design marketing and sales campaigns to attract more of them.

This is a very elementary explanation of this field, which is commonly called database marketing or customer relationship management (CRM), but I want to stress to you that gaining expertise in it is becoming more and more important to stay competitive. While many small businesses remain unsophisticated in this area, the best ones embrace it. It is not going away, and you must master it in order for your kingdom business to be as effective as it can be.

Big companies like the one I work for can afford to employ specialists like my team and me to work in this field full time. As a business owner, you do not have this kind of time to become an expert in each complex piece of this. Even after twenty years in the field, I am not an expert on each piece of software or methodology of quantitative analysis. The good news is that you don't have to be the expert at everything in order to effectively lead your company in this area. I mainly focus on creating an ever-expanding vision of where I want to take my area, and work with my employees closely to make sure we achieve the desired results. They are the real experts on the various software and database technologies. I just make sure I have a working knowledge of the technology. Primarily, I focus on the needs of the business and its customers, and develop vision around those. So far, it has had excellent results.

As an entrepreneur, the same approach is available to you. Fortunately, there is good marketing and sales software available that lets you automate reports and spot trends without having to have the specialized expertise of my team and me. I know of several businesses that have trained proven employees on a good marketing system, and they have learned to produce the reports and perform the analysis necessary for the business owner to make good marketing decisions.

The main point to consider here is that you do not need to be the one who runs the software system or who does the analysis. However, you do need to develop a working knowledge of this important field so you can lead your business and employees in this critically important field. For further reading, I recommend *Duct Tape Marketing*, by John Jantsch, any of Dan Kennedy's marketing books, and, of course, Michael Gerber's book *E-Myth Mastery*.

Sales and Customer Service System

I want to end this section by focusing on sales and customer service. To me, they are intertwined. Returning to the long list of family names in this chapter of Nehemiah, you may recall we discussed God's intimate knowledge of each of His people. He knows our unique needs, and we are precious to Him despite our many flaws because we are adopted into His family through the blood of Christ. I'm not saying you need to adopt your customers into your family, but I am saying that God has given us the model for treating our customers as individuals and being responsive to their individual needs and situations.

What I am not saying is that we should adopt different sets of rules and practices for different customers. That is not the model God has given us. He has not created different means of salvation for different people. Rather, He has created one way of salvation for all people through Jesus Christ. He has created one standard for truth, not several. Nevertheless, within His framework, He addresses our individual needs. So let's not think that just because we build operational systems and standards for our kingdom businesses, these preclude us from meeting the individual needs of customers within the framework we have developed.

In the last section, we discussed the necessity of having a good marketing system. The encounter with the individual customer is the moment of truth for that system. If you have done everything right with your marketing, you know many of the macro characteristics of the customer who is either in your store, on the phone with your call center, or on your Web site. Now the sales process takes over, and you must deliver on their individual needs. Your messages must resonate with them, giving them the feeling that you genuinely understand and care about them.

Why is this important? At the end of the day, we all want to have relationships with people or organizations that know us and treat us fairly and respectfully. Even more, we remain loyal to the organizations with which we have relationships when they go out of their way to provide a consistently high value experience for us. Even if you have a business where you never actually see your customers, such as an Internet business, you can still build relationships with your customers through a number of electronic tools. Regardless of the technology used, customers still want to bond with you, to be treated fairly, and to consistently have a great experience.

When we build our sales and customer service systems so that they are responsive to the needs of individual customers, we are actually modeling God's relationship with us. Modeling God in this way actually brings great glory to Him because we show love for our customers just as He shows loves for us. Furthermore, it also helps differentiate us from the poor to average sales and service people receive from most businesses. For most of these businesses, there are no relationships formed, there are no memorable experiences, and there is no customer loyalty.

Right now I would like you to think about the companies you do business with on a regular basis. My guess is that most of them do not know your name, nor do they keep any record of your transactions with them. If you stop doing business with them tomorrow, they will never know it. They make no effort at all to communicate with you by thanking you for your business or offering you any special promotions or value-added information that would endear you to them. With the technology available today, I feel this is inexcusable. On the other hand, it is a great opportunity for kingdom businesses like yours to rise above the crowd and truly distinguish your business from your competitors.

Remember the motivation for this. Yes, we do it because it is good business and helps make us profitable, and profits are good. More importantly, however, is that we are modeling God's love for us when we go the extra mile to know our customers and provide a consistently excellent experience to create loyalty so they keep coming back.

View From the Trenches: Financial

As I told you earlier, I am neither an accountant, nor a financial analyst by trade, but I am committed to running a profitable business. That's why I have learned to frequently study the Busy Bees financial statements. Fortunately, necessity has made me look deeply into my income statement to ask questions about particular expenses, trying to really understand what we are purchasing and how it is either helping us become more efficient, providing a better quality service, or giving us a competitive advantage. I especially do this with payroll dollars, which account for 67 percent of all our expenses. My questions are not just limited to payroll dollars, though. I ask about classroom expenses, food costs, and maintenance items.

Frequently, what I find is that even our leaders do not have the same profit mentality that we do and, as a result, are more likely to go over budget on things that could potentially be deferred until later. While our managers do an excellent job with the budget, sometimes extraordinary expenses do not get communicated between us, so I have decided to improve our financial communication. To do this, I have developed weekly reports that tell us where we are against our budgeted expenses and revenues. This helps us anticipate future expenses better and also shows us how many budget dollars we have left for a month.

I also find that looking at our income statement and budget frequently provides me with good teaching opportunities for our employees. It is a useful coaching tool to help them understand the company's priorities, and it helps them understand our philosophies in terms of what expenses add value and what do not.

Unfortunately, I was not as strong in the early days of Busy Bees as I am now. Not that I am as strong as I would like to be, but I have improved considerably. As a result of my weakness in this area, much money was wasted. I found that if I did not establish clear priorities for budget expenditures, our employees will set their own priorities, and those priorities are not based on return on investment.

Another major failure early on was not establishing a good financial system with checks and balances. The starting point of this failure was hiring people who barely knew what money was, let alone who could count it. The directors we hired in our earlier days did a poor job with billing and taking payments. As a result, we had many customer delinquencies. Believe it or not, customers don't always pay, even at a Christian preschool. While these directors were flawed in many ways, I still blame myself for not hiring people with more business sense and not designing a simple enough system for them to use.

I hate to admit this, but as a warning to you, I will: There was a period of time when we did not have a budget, and our directors were armed with credit cards. Of course, I knew better than that. I had successfully managed a budget in my corporate job for many years. I had created a detailed pro forma income statement for Busy Bees prior to our opening, so I was aware of financial matters. Here I was, a smart guy who did not take the time to establish a budget. Adding to the nightmare were these credit card-equipped directors with limited financial experience and minimal accountability. This was a recipe for disaster, and that's exactly what happened. The overspending of these directors due to my poor leadership nearly broke us and was one gigantic reason we felt as though we were at the gates of hell.

Don't ask me why I was so lax in this critical area. I know having a full-time job took away my focus, but I think the main reason was that I was naive. I trusted Christian employees to be as frugal with my money as they would be with their own, and failed to give them the guidance and systems they needed to be successful in this area.

By God's grace, we realized the mess we were in and asked my mother and father to help us create good systems. Fortunately for us, my mother agreed to oversee all purchasing, and my father agreed to do our bookkeeping. They were able to create the dual control systems we needed in order to keep our directors on task and accountable in this area. Task number one was removing all access to money from our directors. Now I feel we have a system we can trust. Please don't make the same mistakes I did. Make sure you think through your financial processes, and by all means, be a strong leader.

View From the Trenches: Marketing

Fortunately, I do know a little about marketing, but once again, I spent money on some things that were ineffective. Primarily, I am thinking about radio. For our school, with one brick-and-mortar location, radio is overkill. Its reach is much farther than our physical trade area, and its cost is relatively high. After overspending for months in this area, I decided to return to my roots of direct marketing.

Direct mail has worked somewhat well for us. One approach has been to buy lists of subscribers to parenting magazines and use those in direct mail. We have had some success there. Whenever we have done direct mail, our response rate has been in the neighborhood of 1 percent. Direct mail can be relatively expensive, but I am convinced that it is an essential way to generate leads.

Another way we generate leads is advertising in several print publications directed toward children's services. Those are aimed directly toward our target audience, and we always make sure we create strong offers and give compelling reasons for people to come to our school. We strive hard to tell the reasons we are different, and use as many customer testimonials as we can.

For a marketing software, we use Infusionsoft. It is software built specifically for small businesses, and we have found it very useful. It lets us build personalized, predefined email campaigns for our prospects and customers. For example, we have created a series of six or seven emails we want prospects to receive over an eighteen-day period. Now we simply enter the name of each prospect into the system, and the prospects automatically begin receiving follow-up messages from us. Anytime we want our prospects to receive a follow-up sequence of emails, we simply create the emails and send it to all of them. It is a fairly sophisticated database, but it is relatively easy to use. It has many capabilities we do not yet use, mainly because I am the one using the system. I don't necessarily want to be the one using it, but due to my background, I have wanted to be the system designer and user until I could be sure we had employees with the skill level to use it successfully. I still don't think we are there, although it is a goal we have.

While we don't have all the rich data that a large company has, we still make sure we track certain key marketing items. For example, we always track our lead sources. We know how many come from our Web site, word of mouth, magazines, direct mail, and just by people driving by. We feel tracking this regularly is important to be able to see how effective our marketing dollars are.

At our school, leads generally become prospects when they come to the school for a tour. We like to measure our conversion rate of tours to enrollments so we can know how effective our sales process is. Read more on this in the next section.

We also look at the zip codes and addresses of our customers to see where they are coming from. Doing this has allowed us to eliminate many zip codes from our mailings so that we now focus on about four primary ones.

Another way we analyze data at Busy Bees is through customer surveys. We do this at least twice a year and try to design the survey and questions in such a way that they yield actionable items. This has provided us with very useful feedback, which we have used to improve our operation.

View From the Trenches: Sales and Customer Service

Since I have been sharing horror stories with you, let me share another one involving sales. By now, you should assume that our directors, who are our primary sales people, lacked enough knowledge about sales. They are smart people in general, but ill-equipped for sales. Through my weekly meetings and intense questioning, I found out from one of our now departed directors that her sales process for inquiring prospects was fairly impersonal and standardized. She told the prospects what we did at the school, but never established a questioning process that revealed what was important to the potential customer. Also, she would allow the prospects to leave the facility without giving us their contact information. So not only had she given an impersonal tour; she also had eliminated any possibility for follow-up.

We quickly designed and established a new mandatory process where the prospect enters the facility and fills out her contact information as well as a brief questionnaire where she can rate different elements of a preschool in terms of importance to her. During this brief interview, we also get to know her as well as her child a little bit. The director then gives the prospect a tour, stopping in the classroom where the child would attend if enrolled. The director gives the survey to the teacher, who can explain what is done in the classroom according to what the parent has indicated is important to her. This is much more personalized selling and has resulted in much more effective tours.

Another personalized aspect of our sales and customer service system is the one-on-one time our children have daily with their teachers. Each child has five to ten minutes of individualized attention with his teacher each day, and this greatly helps the teachers in addressing the needs of each child. We also use daily and weekly progress sheets, which allow the parents to see the progress of their child in different aspects of their learning, such as math, social development, Bible, and so on. Finally, periodic parent-teacher conferences help parents and teachers to build relationships with each other as well as get both parties focused on the specific needs of individual children.

Cindy and I, who are not at the school every day, develop relationships with our customers through periodic open houses, monthly newsletters, value-added emails on pertinent topics such as parenting tips, and phone calls in the evenings to check customer satisfaction levels and let them know how much we appreciate their business.

While we still have many things to improve upon, I hope this section has shown you that even in a small business such as a preschool, there are still many ways that quantitative analysis and personalized sales and customer service can be utilized. You will stand out from the crowd if you build these into your business, and you will be modeling God's principles of accounting and providing loving individualized attention that are demonstrated to us in Nehemiah chapter 7.

Chapter 12

God's Recognition of Faithful Kingdom Service: Nehemiah 7:70-73

Each one's work will become manifest, for the Day will disclose it, because it will be revealed by fire, and the fire will test what sort of work each one has done. If the work that anyone has built on the foundation survives, he will receive a reward.

1 Corinthians 3:13-14

At the end of this very long chapter 7 of Nehemiah, we see him note the contributions of God's people to the work of rebuilding the walls and city. Let's read the passage and then see how we can apply it to our kingdom businesses.

[70]Now some of the heads of fathers' houses gave to the work. The governor gave to the treasury 1,000 darics of gold, 50 basins, 30 priests' garments and 500 minas of silver. [71]And some of the heads of fathers' houses gave into the treasury of the work 20,000 darics of gold and 2,200 minas of silver. [72]And what the rest of the people gave was 20,000 darics of gold, 2,000 minas of silver, and 67 priests' garments. [73]So the priests, the Levites, the gatekeepers, the singers, some of the people, the temple servants, and all Israel, lived in their towns.

It is interesting that the contributions were itemized according to the governor, the heads of the fathers' houses, and the rest of the people. All in all, here is how the contributions to the treasury were broken down:

Type of Person	Gold Drachmas	Basins	Priestly Garments	Silver Minas
Governor	1,000	50	530	
Heads of Fathers' Households	20,000			2,200
Rest of People	20,000		67	2,000
Total	41,000	50	597	4,200

In chapter 3 of Nehemiah, we discussed the topic of recognizing people for their work toward God's kingdom, and here the topic arises again because as entrepreneurs and leaders, we need to hear it over and over again. In this instance, different groups of people, from the governor down to the common people, are sacrificing part of their limited resources for the work of rebuilding Jerusalem so God's kingdom could grow and prosper. Continuing with the theme of God's accounting standards, these verses tell us He knows exactly what each person does for His kingdom, and like 1 Corinthians 3 says, our work will be tested by fire. If our work is found to be built on the solid foundation of Jesus Christ, it will endure and be rewarded.

Not only is this a reminder to build our kingdom business on Jesus Christ all the time, but it also reminds us that our sovereign and all-powerful God is intimately acquainted with our work for His kingdom. None of us want to be like the person described in 1 Corinthians 3:15, whose work is burned up, suffers loss, and barely makes it into God's kingdom. The fact that our God is closely watching and testing what we do should be great motivation for all of us to work for His glory each day, carefully examining our hearts and motivations as we make decisions in our businesses.

To me, one of the most interesting aspects of this particular passage is the fact that the heads of the fathers' households and the rest of the people contributed so much more to the work than the governor. On a per capita basis, Nehemiah the governor, no doubt, contributed more than the other people. Nevertheless, the contributions of the two other people groups were approximately forty times greater than the governor. What does that tell us?

It is a stark depiction of the contributions of our employees to our business compared to our own, and shows us how dependent we are on them. There is no doubt that you and I as kingdom entrepreneurs throw our lives into our businesses and invest bucketfuls of time and money. Far and away, we have the highest per capita contribution of resources compared to any of our employees. Despite this, the contributions you and I make as entrepreneurs, though important and recognized by God, are trivial compared to the contributions of our employees.

How do our employees sacrifice and contribute? Primarily through their time, but also occasionally through their own financial resources. If you work sixty hours a week in your business, and you have five employees each working forty hours per week, they still put in 233 percent more hours than you. Our businesses stand no chance of growing unless we have excellent employees who work in them and do their best every day. This is not to diminish the work you and I do as leaders because without us, there would be no business. Consider Nehemiah. Without him, this massive undertaking would not have gotten under way. However, you and I know that if we are doing our jobs properly, the bulk of the output of our businesses will be created by our employees.

This, of course, put a huge burden on us as leaders, as we have already discussed. If we are to have employees contributing like these Israelites did, we have to hire the right ones in the first place and have training and compensation mechanisms in place that continue to challenge and motivate them. Of course, most of all, you have to show an interest in them as well as continually share your vision with them.

God recognizes the contributions of the people who work for us, and He has some warnings for us as leaders in how we think of and treat our employees. In Ephesians 6:9, the apostle Paul tells us to do good to our employees and not threaten them. He says, "knowing that he who is both their Master and yours is in heaven, and that there is no partiality with him." Just because we are in charge of our company does not mean we do not have a boss. The Scripture clearly states that we answer to God. God doesn't value us as entrepreneurs any more highly than he does the people who work for us. He has made us to have different gifts than our employees, and He has also given them different gifts than we have. This is a call to humility and teamwork, recognizing that we, owners and employees alike, are all working on the same kingdom team for the same kingdom purpose.

If we need any more clarification on how God thinks of us and our employees, we should consider the following passage from 1 Corinthians 12:7-27:

> [7]To each is given the manifestation of the Spirit for the common good. [8]For to one is given through the Spirit the utterance of wisdom, and to another the utterance of knowledge according to the same Spirit, [9]to another faith by the same Spirit, to another gifts of healing by the one Spirit, [10]to another the working of miracles, to another prophecy, to another the ability to distinguish between spirits, to another various kinds of tongues, to another the interpretation of tongues. [11]All these are empowered by one and the same Spirit, who apportions to each one individually as he wills.
>
> [12]For just as the body is one and has many members, and all the members of the body, though many, are one body, so it is with Christ. [13]For in one Spirit we were all baptized into one body—Jews or Greeks, slaves or free—and all were made to drink of one Spirit.
>
> [14]For the body does not consist of one member but of many. [15]If the foot should say, "Because I am not a hand, I do not belong to the body," that would not make it any less a part of the body. [16]And if the ear should say, "Because I am not an eye, I do not belong to the body," that would not make it any less a part of the body. [17]If the whole body were an eye, where would be the sense of hearing? If the whole body were an ear, where would be the sense of smell? [18]But as it

is, God arranged the members in the body, each one of them, as he chose. [19]If all were a single member, where would the body be? [20]As it is, there are many parts, yet one body.

[21]The eye cannot say to the hand, "I have no need of you," nor again the head to the feet, "I have no need of you." [22]On the contrary, the parts of the body that seem to be weaker are indispensable, [23]and on those parts of the body that we think less honorable we bestow the greater honor, and our unpresentable parts are treated with greater modesty, [24]which our more presentable parts do not require. But God has so composed the body, giving greater honor to the part that lacked it, [25]that there may be no division in the body, but that the members may have the same care for one another. [26]If one member suffers, all suffer together; if one member is honored, all rejoice together.

[27]Now you are the body of Christ and individually members of it.

Applying these verses to a kingdom business, nothing could be clearer than the fact that we and our employees are part of the body of Christ. If it is so clear that God considers us and our employees equal in Christ, why is it that so many entrepreneurs often neglect their employees and treat them with disdain? Consider this extraordinarily harsh warning from James 5:1-6:

[1]Come now, you rich, weep and howl for the miseries that are coming upon you. [2]Your riches have rotted and your garments are moth-eaten. [3]Your gold and silver have corroded, and their corrosion will be evidence against you and will eat your flesh like fire. You have laid up treasure in the last days. [4]Behold, the wages of the laborers who mowed your fields, which you kept back by fraud, are crying out against you, and the cries of the harvesters have reached the ears of the Lord of hosts. [5]You have lived on the earth in luxury and in self-indulgence. You have fattened your hearts in a day of slaughter. [6]You have condemned and murdered the righteous person. He does not resist you.

If we run our businesses with excellence, and if the Lord blesses them, there is a good chance we will become financially prosperous. This passage is telling us not to let ourselves be corrupted by that prosperity. Instead of hoarding all our profits for ourselves, James is calling us to fairness toward our employees and appreciation for their efforts. Of course, this translates to providing fair human resource policies, such as vacations, sick pay, and whatever other benefits we can truly afford. Certainly, incentive payments and profit sharing can be part of this mix. In addition, I believe it entails providing our high-performing employees opportunities to better themselves through education and increasingly challenging opportunities at work.

All in all, God is showing us in these last few verses of Nehemiah chapter 7 that He is grateful for the contributions made by our entire team, not just the entrepreneur or top management. Because we are called to model our lives after Him, He wants us to be humble and take note of the many contributions of our employees and reward them with fair compensation, benefits, recognition, and opportunities to improve themselves. It is almost as if He has given us a "flock" of people to care for from a work and career standpoint, and He wants to make sure we take care of them. I don't mean that from a socialistic perspective, as in a caretaker. If they want to work for us, they definitely need to earn their rewards. However, we are called to love our neighbor as ourselves, and that is the message God is conveying to us about our employees. We are definitely in the people development business.

View From the Trenches

Neither Cindy nor I have worked one minute at Busy Bees in the capacity of cooking meals, teaching children, creating reports, calling parents of sick children, cleaning toilets, or changing diapers. We spend maybe nine hours per month in meetings with employees and maybe another three to six hours per week in the evenings. So altogether, we work about twenty-five to thirty hours per month, or about seven hours per week, on average.

On the other hand, Busy Bees is open eleven hours each weekday. That translates to at least seven hundred labor hours per week worked by our employees. The time they spend contributing to our business is at least one hundred times greater than ours. They are the ones who really make the business successful. They are the ones the parents and children build relationships with and rave about. That's not to say that Cindy and I are unimportant. Without God's working through us, there would be no Busy Bees, and our employees would not have a Christian preschool to work for. In addition, Cindy and I fund every penny of Busy Bees, something that has great importance.

Nevertheless, Cindy and I are primarily in the background, and our employees get the credit. We are perfectly happy for things to go on this way. We don't need or want the credit. Rather, we know if our employees succeed, we will succeed as well.

From a reward and recognition standpoint of our employees, we try to acknowledge strong performance by giving our existing employees preference when a higher-level job opens up. In addition, we offer an above-market wage. Unfortunately, we cannot afford a true benefits package at this point, but it is our goal to add profit sharing, retirement contributions, and educational assistance when it is financially prudent to do so.

As a startup business, it has been hard to offer our employees all the incentives and rewards they deserve for excellent performance because profits have been so minimal. It is awkward to be in the position where you want to reward someone who has gone above and beyond, but you are unable to do so because your revenues are so squeezed. That's why we make sure to pay well compared to other preschools, and we provide gifts and a special home-cooked meal for them at Christmastime.

Most importantly, though, is the fact that we pray for our employees and spend time with them individually. We know that God sees and appreciates their contributions to His kingdom every day, and this gives us motivation to appreciate them as well.

Chapter 13

The Kingdom Vision Begins to Bear Fruit: Nehemiah Chapter 8

You did not choose me, but I chose you and appointed you that you should go and bear fruit and that your fruit should abide, so that whatever you ask the Father in my name, he may give it to you.

John 15:16

U p to this point, we have focused most of our attention on the construction of the wall. In chapter 7, Nehemiah tells us that it was finished. After completing the wall, we see Nehemiah immediately begin focusing on his ultimate goal, that of repopulating the city with God-fearing Israelites. We know he thought of the construction project as a means to revitalize God's people into a strong nation once again, one that worshiped God and was faithful to Him. In chapter 8 of Nehemiah, we see evidence of his goal being reached.

As we study this chapter, I would like you to consider the ultimate purpose of your kingdom business. It is more than just wall building, right? The wall represents the products and services you and I create and sell, but you and I want to go beyond that. As kingdom business leaders and entrepreneurs, we seek the same thing Nehemiah sought—the impact, the significance achieved for the kingdom. In the Scripture below this chapter's heading, Jesus says He appointed us to go and bear fruit, and that our fruit should remain. The walls of our businesses may fall down some day, but what will really matter is our fruit. Nehemiah's fruit remains to this day, just as Jesus said. Why should the fruit of our kingdom businesses be any different? Here is Nehemiah chapter 8:

[1]And all the people gathered as one man into the square before the Water Gate. And they told Ezra the scribe to bring the Book of the Law of Moses that the LORD had commanded Israel. [2]So Ezra the priest brought the Law before the assembly, both men and women and all who could understand what they heard, on the first day of the seventh month. [3]And he read from it facing the square before the Water Gate from early morning until midday, in the presence of the men and the women and those who could understand. And the ears of all the people were attentive to the Book of the Law. [4]And Ezra the scribe stood on a wooden platform that they had made for the purpose. And beside him stood Mattithiah, Shema, Anaiah, Uriah, Hilkiah, and Maaseiah on his right hand, and Pedaiah, Mishael, Malchijah, Hashum, Hashbaddanah, Zechariah, and Meshullam on his left hand. [5]And Ezra opened the book in the sight of all the people, for he was above all the people, and as he opened it all the people stood. [6]And Ezra blessed the LORD, the great God, and all the people answered, "Amen, Amen," lifting up their hands. And they bowed their heads and worshiped the LORD with their faces to the ground. [7]Also Jeshua, Bani, Sherebiah, Jamin, Akkub, Shabbethai, Hodiah, Maaseiah, Kelita, Azariah, Jozabad, Hanan, Pelaiah, the Levites, helped the people to understand the Law, while the people remained in their places. [8]They read from the book, from the Law of God, clearly, and they gave the sense, so that the people understood the reading.

[9]And Nehemiah, who was the governor, and Ezra the priest and scribe, and the Levites who taught the people said to all the people, "This day is holy to the LORD your God; do not mourn or weep." For all the people wept as they heard the words of the Law. [10]Then he said to them, "Go your way.

Eat the fat and drink sweet wine and send portions to anyone who has nothing ready, for this day is holy to our Lord. And do not be grieved, for the joy of the LORD is your strength." [11]So the Levites calmed all the people, saying, "Be quiet, for this day is holy; do not be grieved." [12]And all the people went their way to eat and drink and to send portions and to make great rejoicing, because they had understood the words that were declared to them.

[13]On the second day, the heads of fathers' houses of all the people, with the priests and the Levites, came together to Ezra the scribe in order to study the words of the Law. [14]And they found it written in the Law that the LORD had commanded by Moses that the people of Israel should dwell in booths during the feast of the seventh month, [15]and that they should proclaim it and publish it in all their towns and in Jerusalem, "Go out to the hills and bring branches of olive, wild olive, myrtle, palm, and other leafy trees to make booths, as it is written." [16]So the people went out and brought them and made booths for themselves, each on his roof, and in their courts and in the courts of the house of God, and in the square at the Water Gate and in the square at the Gate of Ephraim. [17]And all the assembly of those who had returned from the captivity made booths and lived in the booths, for from the days of Jeshua the son of Nun to that day the people of Israel had not done so. And there was very great rejoicing. [18]And day by day, from the first day to the last day, he read from the Book of the Law of God. They kept the feast seven days, and on the eighth day there was a solemn assembly, according to the rule.

What occurred here, I believe, is exactly what Nehemiah envisioned when he was way back in Shushan, pondering and praying about how he was going to help his people rise out of their miserable condition. My God grant that you and I can see similar results with our businesses.

In these verses, the people assembled together to give glory to God for the completion of the wall. This was not an elaborate worship service like the one we will discuss in Nehemiah chapter 12, but this simple service consisted of reading and teaching God's Word from morning until midday.

We see the preeminence and power of God's Word in this worship service as well as in the discipling of the heads of households that occurred later in the chapter. As Ezra read the Word, the Levites helped the people understand its meaning. From their response of mourning and weeping upon hearing the Word, I have to believe that for many of these people, it was the first time they had heard God's Word in a long time. Remember, they had been living interspersed with the peoples of different nations, so it is safe to assume they had neglected God's Word as they absorbed other cultures and belief systems into their lives. I believe the weeping and mourning came from being convicted that they had wandered far from God. The prayer of confession we will study in Nehemiah chapter 9 supports this position.

When the leaders saw the reaction of the people, they intervened to say, "Don't be sad. This is a day of great rejoicing." They realized what God had done for them by rebuilding the wall and resurrecting their nation, and they wanted the people to understand it as well. Once the people understood the true meaning of what was said to them from God's Word, they went away happy.

In the second part of the chapter, we see the heads of the families return to Ezra so they can understand more of God's Word. As they gained an understanding of God's Word, they went home and taught it to their families. In response to the discipling by the heads of their families, their families obeyed God and had great joy from rededicating their lives to Him. What a tremendous picture this is of God's design for families. It reminds us of the passage in Deuteronomy 6:4-9, which says:

Hear, O Israel: The LORD our God, the LORD is one. You shall love the LORD your God with all your heart and with all your soul and with all your might. And these words that I command you today shall be on your heart. You shall teach them diligently to your children, and shall talk of them when you sit in your house, and when you walk by the way, and when you lie down, and when you rise. You shall bind them as a sign on your hand, and they shall be as frontlets between your eyes. You shall write them on the doorposts of your house and on your gates.

In God's kingdom, the primary responsibility for discipling children lies with parents. For those of us who are parents, discipling our children is one of our top priorities in addition to loving God, caring for our spouse, and providing for our families. Unfortunately, training our families in God's ways can sometimes get neglected. Here in this chapter we are shown the powerful impact of parents being discipled in God's Word by a more mature believer. This gave them the spiritual fuel they needed to positively impact their families.

From a broader perspective, this chapter shows us the tremendous importance of making God's Word available to people, as well as the utter necessity of having leaders and teachers available who can help those with less knowledge and maturity correctly understand the Word. God's Word is so powerful, much more so than we can possibly imagine. You and I know it contains the story of Jesus Christ. It is how His work of redemption is communicated to us and how we know our lives have meaning.

So now that we have an understanding of this chapter, how can we apply it to our businesses? Remember, the events of this chapter were what Nehemiah envisioned as a result of the walls being built. If we take the same approach as entrepreneurs, we are ultimately led back to desiring that our work will result in somebody somewhere being called out of darkness into the light of Jesus Christ through the reading and proclamation of God's Word.

If you have a veterinary clinic, auto body shop, or hardware store, does that mean you have to be like Ezra and read God's Word to all your customers? I don't think so. However, you can support the ministry of the Word by doing several things.

First, make sure you are in a good church that faithfully proclaims God's Word and that has good teachers. If you are spiritually dry as the leader of the kingdom business, what do you think will happen to it? It will lose its vision and become like any other secular business.

The demands on you are great, and you need a clear understanding of God's Word to enable you to meet all your challenges.

Second, you can become a discipler yourself. Remember, you are in the people development business, so one way to do this is to hold Bible studies for your employees or customers, or recommend a good church to them. Maybe make the Word available in your office or place of business for people to read as they are waiting.

Third, with your kingdom capital, you can support ministries that take God's Word to the nations. That does not mean that we make it a goal to fund only church entities or missionaries, although those are certainly outstanding ways to invest our capital. It does mean that we seek to invest our capital in places where God's Word will have a place of preeminence and reverence. For example, if Cindy and I were to support a hospital or academic scholarship, we would look for places that had a high regard for God's Word and that made it accessible to its patients or students.

One key question all of us have to ask is, How will we know when we have achieved our goals? Nehemiah could see that much of his goal was beginning to be fulfilled here in chapter 8. The people would still have many hard trials to come, but at least they were in a much stronger position than previously and had started to return to God.

How will you know when your kingdom goals will start to bear fruit? I suggest that you will know when you see people reading and understanding God's Word as a result of the work you perform.

View From the Trenches

This is the fun part of Busy Bees Christian PreSchool. We have the luxury of being able to proclaim God's Word every day as part of our business. We are very upfront about this with every prospective customer. This is who we are. It's in our name.

For our students, we proclaim God's Word to them every day through Bible stories, memory verses, songs, craft activities, and a children's catechism. Some of our most encouraging moments have come from parents who have remarked that their children tell them Bible stories at home or participate in the Lord's Prayer during church services. Not all of our students come from Christian families. I estimate that maybe 50 percent or 60 percent do. For the rest of them, we may be the only place these children ever hear God's Word. We think about these little kids learning about Jesus, and pray that God will water those seeds we plant so they can grow up to become followers of Christ and outstanding members of society. In Isaiah 55:11, God says His Word will not return to Him void, so we have great hope that He will build upon what we are teaching our students.

For our employees, we read and discuss God's Word in our team meetings, training sessions, and informal one-on-one meetings. Recently, our director began a Bible study for our employees, and I can see a tremendous difference at the school. We have quite a few people working for us who are relatively new Christians and have limited experience with God's Word. We purchased a great Bible study course from Ligonier Ministries called "From Dust to Glory," and the employees are excited to be studying God's Word with their friends.

As for Cindy and I, we faithfully attend a good church and lead two Bible studies there, as well as a children's ministry. We spend time in the Word ourselves, and we also have family worship where we study God's Word with our children. Is everything we do the "right way"? Do we have all the answers? Absolutely not. We have our struggles just like anyone else. However, we are happy that God's Word is held in high esteem in our business and family.

Have we achieved all our goals? No way. We are just beginning. We envision at least four or five preschools, at least one private Christian school, and potentially additional Web-based training for children and adults. We also want to be able to completely fund new church startups as well as provide increasingly large levels of support to missionaries. For now, we are happy that God is using us and our business to spread His Word.

Chapter 14

The Kingdom People Confess Their Sins and Declare God's Mercy: Nehemiah Chapter 9

If we say we have no sin, we deceive ourselves, and the truth is not in us. If we confess our sins, he is faithful and just to forgive us our sins and to cleanse us from all unrighteousness. If we say we have not sinned, we make him a liar, and his word is not in us.

1 John 1:8-10

As believers, we know that sin entered into the world when Adam and Eve made their fatal and tragic decisions in the Garden of Eden. Ever since then, all of us have been corrupted by sin. Romans chapter 3 gives a brutal account of this, saying in verses 10-12: "As it is written: 'None is righteous, no, not one; no one understands; no one seeks for God. All have turned aside; together they have become worthless; no one does good, not even one.'"

Those of us who have given our lives to the Lord Jesus Christ are saved by grace and by God's Holy Spirit living in us are growing more like Christ each day. However, we all know that we are far from sinless. We are like the apostle Paul, who cries out in frustration at his own sinfulness, saying in Romans 7:21-25: "So I find it to be a law that when I want to do right, evil lies close at hand.

For I delight in the law of God, in my inner being, but I see in my members another law waging war against the law of my mind and making me captive to the law of sin that dwells in my members. Wretched man that I am! Who will deliver me from this body of death? Thanks be to God through Jesus Christ our Lord! So then, I myself serve the law of God with my mind, but with my flesh I serve the law of sin."

What does all this have to do with a business book? Very simply, since you and I, as well as our employees and customers, are sinners, sin is going to happen in our businesses. As Nehemiah has already demonstrated to us through the behavior of the Israelites, we can expect jealousy, divisions, bickering, pride, and a host of other sins. You may even find sins involving sexual immorality, fraud or embezzlement, theft, or substance abuse. Human beings are pretty creative when it comes to disobeying God. There's just about nothing they can't think of.

Sin is real, and it is going to occur within your business. You yourself will sin and will also be a victim of the sin of others. The only question is, What will you do about it? There is only one right way to deal with it, and that is to confess it and ask for forgiveness. Read the Scripture again under the title of this chapter. John tells us we are sinners, and that we are liars if we try to deny it. He commands us to confess our sins, and promises that God will cleanse us from all unrighteousness through the blood of Jesus Christ.

In this ninth chapter of Nehemiah, we find the people once again assembled in a worship service where they are praising and worshiping the Lord. One aspect of this worship that was not mentioned in the service in chapter 8 is confession of sin. In this service, the confession of their collective sin as a people took a very long time. In fact, this prayer of confession is the longest prayer in the entire Old Testament. Let's read it, then apply it.

[1]Now on the twenty-fourth day of this month the people of Israel were assembled with fasting and in sackcloth, and with earth on their heads. [2]And the Israelites separated themselves from all foreigners and stood and confessed their sins and the iniquities of their fathers. [3] And they stood up in

their place and read from the Book of the Law of the LORD their God for a quarter of the day; for another quarter of it they made confession and worshiped the LORD their God. [4]On the stairs of the Levites stood Jeshua, Bani, Kadmiel, Shebaniah, Bunni, Sherebiah, Bani, and Chenani; and they cried with a loud voice to the LORD their God. [5]Then the Levites, Jeshua, Kadmiel, Bani, Hashabneiah, Sherebiah, Hodiah, Shebaniah, and Pethahiah, said, "Stand up and bless the LORD your God from everlasting to everlasting. Blessed be your glorious name, which is exalted above all blessing and praise.

[6]"You are the LORD, you alone. You have made heaven, the heaven of heavens, with all their host, the earth and all that is on it, the seas and all that is in them; and you preserve all of them; and the host of heaven worships you. [7]You are the LORD, the God who chose Abram and brought him out of Ur of the Chaldeans and gave him the name Abraham. [8]You found his heart faithful before you, and made with him the covenant to give to his offspring the land of the Canaanite, the Hittite, the Amorite, the Perizzite, the Jebusite, and the Girgashite. And you have kept your promise, for you are righteous.

[9]"And you saw the affliction of our fathers in Egypt and heard their cry at the Red Sea, [10]and performed signs and wonders against Pharaoh and all his servants and all the people of his land, for you knew that they acted arrogantly against our fathers. And you made a name for yourself, as it is to this day. [11]And you divided the sea before them, so that they went through the midst of the sea on dry land, and you cast their pursuers into the depths, as a stone into mighty waters. [12]By a pillar of cloud you led them in the day, and by a pillar of fire in the night to light for them the way in which they should go. [13]You came down on Mount Sinai and spoke with them from heaven and gave them right rules and true laws, good statutes and commandments, [14]and you made known to them your holy Sabbath and commanded them commandments and statutes and a law by Moses your

servant. [15]You gave them bread from heaven for their hunger and brought water for them out of the rock for their thirst, and you told them to go in to possess the land that you had sworn to give them.

[16]"But they and our fathers acted presumptuously and stiffened their neck and did not obey your commandments. [17]They refused to obey and were not mindful of the wonders that you performed among them, but they stiffened their neck and appointed a leader to return to their slavery in Egypt. But you are a God ready to forgive, gracious and merciful, slow to anger and abounding in steadfast love, and did not forsake them. [18]Even when they had made for themselves a golden calf and said, 'This is your God who brought you up out of Egypt,' and had committed great blasphemies, [19]you in your great mercies did not forsake them in the wilderness. The pillar of cloud to lead them in the way did not depart from them by day, nor the pillar of fire by night to light for them the way by which they should go. [20]You gave your good Spirit to instruct them and did not withhold your manna from their mouth and gave them water for their thirst. [21]Forty years you sustained them in the wilderness, and they lacked nothing. Their clothes did not wear out and their feet did not swell.

[22]"And you gave them kingdoms and peoples and allotted to them every corner. So they took possession of the land of Sihon king of Heshbon and the land of Og king of Bashan. [23]You multiplied their children as the stars of heaven, and you brought them into the land that you had told their fathers to enter and possess. [24]So the descendants went in and possessed the land, and you subdued before them the inhabitants of the land, the Canaanites, and gave them into their hand, with their kings and the peoples of the land, that they might do with them as they would. [25]And they captured fortified cities and a rich land, and took possession of houses full of all good things, cisterns already hewn, vineyards, olive orchards and fruit trees in abundance. So they ate and were

filled and became fat and delighted themselves in your great goodness.

[26]"Nevertheless, they were disobedient and rebelled against you and cast your law behind their back and killed your prophets, who had warned them in order to turn them back to you, and they committed great blasphemies. [27]Therefore you gave them into the hand of their enemies, who made them suffer. And in the time of their suffering they cried out to you and you heard them from heaven, and according to your great mercies you gave them saviors who saved them from the hand of their enemies. [28]But after they had rest they did evil again before you, and you abandoned them to the hand of their enemies, so that they had dominion over them. Yet when they turned and cried to you, you heard from heaven, and many times you delivered them according to your mercies. [29]And you warned them in order to turn them back to your law. Yet they acted presumptuously and did not obey your commandments, but sinned against your rules, which if a person does them, he shall live by them, and they turned a stubborn shoulder and stiffened their neck and would not obey. [30]Many years you bore with them and warned them by your Spirit through your prophets. Yet they would not give ear. Therefore you gave them into the hand of the peoples of the lands. [31]Nevertheless, in your great mercies you did not make an end of them or forsake them, for you are a gracious and merciful God.

[32]"Now, therefore, our God, the great, the mighty, and the awesome God, who keeps covenant and steadfast love, let not all the hardship seem little to you that has come upon us, upon our kings, our princes, our priests, our prophets, our fathers, and all your people, since the time of the kings of Assyria until this day. [33]Yet you have been righteous in all that has come upon us, for you have dealt faithfully and we have acted wickedly. [34]Our kings, our princes, our priests, and our fathers have not kept your law or paid attention to your commandments and your warnings that you gave them. [35]Even in their own kingdom, and amid your great goodness

that you gave them, and in the large and rich land that you set before them, they did not serve you or turn from their wicked works. [36]Behold, we are slaves this day; in the land that you gave to our fathers to enjoy its fruit and its good gifts, behold, we are slaves. [37]And its rich yield goes to the kings whom you have set over us because of our sins. They rule over our bodies and over our livestock as they please, and we are in great distress.

[38]"Because of all this we make a firm covenant in writing; on the sealed document are the names of our princes, our Levites, and our priests."

This prayer actually has four aspects to it. They are: adoration, confession, thanksgiving, and supplication. They adore God by praising Him in the beginning of the prayer, acknowledging His glory, majesty, omnipotence, and mercy. Notice how they focus on God's name by saying, "Blessed be your glorious name." This is reminiscent of the third commandment and the Lord's Prayer, both of which remind us to use God's name carefully and honorably. Since God cares so much about how His name is used, this makes us think about how we use God's name in our businesses. Are we using it in a way that is honoring Him and that acknowledges His sovereignty and mercy?

The second element of the prayer is confession. What was the major sin that occurred over and over again throughout the history of Israel? It was the sin of arrogance and pride, leading to disobedience. Time after time, God blessed the people abundantly, and time after time, they became arrogant and detached from God as a result of those blessings. In short, the great prosperity given to them by God made them so prideful that they actually began to believe they had acquired it on their own, independent of God. Instead of using their prosperity to be a blessing to others as a way to thank God, their own prosperity became their god so that they followed the "rules of prosperity" instead of God's rules. This caused them to drift away from God to the point where they abandoned Him altogether and became pagans. Amazingly, the people who were blessed the most by God ended up furthest away from Him.

How does this apply to our kingdom businesses? Almost in more ways than can be counted. First let me speak to much of modern-day as well as historic business literature. I read books upon books from many great business authors, most of who are not Christian. They have excellent principles, and I try to apply them through a Christian filter. I certainly encourage you to be an avid reader of all types of business literature. One type of literature I try to view with particular skepticism and alertness are books that promise instant or easy fortunes by following a few simple steps. In other words, I perceive this literature to focus almost exclusively on getting rich as an end in itself.

Remember, I am a capitalist and like making lots of money. Nevertheless, I think if we are not careful as kingdom business owners, some of the literature out there can get us focused on riches as the end result instead of riches to build God's kingdom. This is the trouble Israel fell into consistently. Time after time, the Bible warns us not to strive too hard to acquire wealth, with even Jesus stating that it is "easier for a camel to go through the eye of a needle than for a rich man to get to heaven." Riches are not bad, but the Bible gives us very strong warnings that let us know that they can corrupt us terminally if they take the place of God in our lives. As our businesses prosper, we have a responsibility to pray for humility and the ability to use God's blessings to build His kingdom instead of letting the prosperity become our idol. Watch out for complacency in yourself and your people.

The next element of confession is to make it specific. The prayer speaks to different historic periods of blessing and sin during Israel's history leading up to the destruction of Jerusalem and the ensuing Babylonian captivity. This prayer lists the sins in each historic period and confesses them. Likewise, in our businesses, we ought to confess our sins specifically, first to God, then to whomever we have harmed. Be quick to apologize as well as forgive. Be the model in this regard. Pride has no place in your kingdom business, so do not let it. First Corinthians 5:6 says, "A little leaven leavens the whole lump." This means even small unconfessed sins can lead to great damage in your kingdom organization. I encourage you to take the lead in this regard and encourage your people to follow.

This entire discussion of confession assumes that you and I are able to recognize sin in our companies. It should be obvious when we see it, but we do not always see it. It can be hidden within our organizations in ways that we might never know about. One biblical example of this occurs in the book of Joshua. After an incredible victory over Jericho, Israel was defeated at the hands of Ai. This defeat occurred because of the sin of one man, Achan. Joshua was not initially aware of this sin. All he knew was that his people had been defeated, and he was sick about it. God pointed out Achan's sin to Joshua and told him this was why they had been defeated. At God's command, Joshua then dealt severely with Achan, and Israel went on to further victory.

Now, by no means am I suggesting we stone anyone for their sins, but we can learn some important lessons from this example in the book of Joshua. The first is that God does not take sin lightly in our businesses. He can withhold blessings, and even bring defeat, due to unexposed sin. Think of the fact that the entire nation of Israel was impacted by the sins of one man. In fact, thirty-six families lost their fathers as a result of the sins of one person. God cares deeply about the sins in our businesses.

Continuing with our examination of the Joshua example, the fact that he was ignorant of the sin due to the huge number of people in Israel gives us a clue as to what we should be looking for and praying about. We ought to be praying that God would expose the sins of our company to us, and can put in place mechanisms through our leadership structure that would help bring these to light.

The final piece of this example is that we need to deal with sin. We cannot turn a blind eye to it. We have already seen Nehemiah deal with sin very forcefully in Nehemiah chapter 5, and we will see it again in Nehemiah chapter 13. Conversely, in 1 Corinthians, the church was admonished for not only letting sin exist, but being proud of it. Scripture tells us to deal with sin, and you and I, as the leaders of our companies, need to be prepared to handle it. Now, we acknowledge we are not the church. We live in a secular society and, in most instances, have to be careful we are not violating laws by forcing our employees to follow Christian rules. Nevertheless, sins such as substance abuse, verbal abuse, lying, fraud, and so on, are still terminable offenses at this point.

The third element of the prayer is what I see as thanksgiving. They did not specifically use the words "thank you," but by pointing to the incredible blessings God showered upon them, in my opinion, they are showing thanksgiving. At the very least, they are confessing their ungratefulness and acknowledging that they should have been thankful. The parts of this prayer that are astonishing to me are the number of times God heard the cries of the people after they had sinned, and had mercy on them. This is epitomized in Nehemiah 9:31, which says, "In your great mercies you did not make an end of them or forsake them, for you are a gracious and merciful God." This verse is ultimately fulfilled by God's showing His greatest mercy by providing Jesus Christ for our sins. Ephesians 2:4-5 tells us, "But God, being rich in mercy, because of the great love with which he loved us, even when we were dead in our trespasses, made us alive together with Christ."

Let me ask you a question: Brother or sister in the Lord, fellow kingdom capitalist, do you recognize the blessings that occur in your business as coming from the Lord? Can you go back and list the blessings God has given your business just like the people outlined God's blessings toward Israel in this prayer? Assuming you recognized God's blessings, how have you responded to them? In pride and arrogance as Israel did, or in humility as Christ wants us to? Are there times when you have gone far astray, ignoring and disobeying God? He has been merciful and brought you back, has He not? If you look closely at the history of your business, not through rose-colored glasses, but impartially, my guess is you will see a similar pattern as Israel experienced. Lead your business in recognizing God's blessings and in being thankful to Him.

The fourth element of Israel's prayer was supplication. That simply means asking God for things with the right motives. We are strongly encouraged throughout Scripture to ask God for things ranging from our daily bread to the desires of our heart. Jesus Himself tells us to ask for anything in His name, not with wrong motives, as the book of James points out, but with a mind toward good things that bring glory to God.

What did Israel ask for? Something very big. They were basically asking God to not forget them, but rather to deliver them from the oppression of the surrounding nations. They wanted to once again return Israel to a thriving, powerful nation that worshiped the Lord.

What big things are you asking the Lord for, and are you doing it with right motives? Have you confessed and dealt with sin, and are you acknowledging God as the mighty King, using His name with reverence? God is prepared to do big things in and through our business, bigger things than we can even ask or think about. But we need to ask for those things in faith.

The final key element of the prayer is found beginning in verse 38, where the leaders make a covenant, or contract, with God. This, in my opinion, is the equivalent of the theological term "repentance," which means turning from our sinful ways and following Christ. It is a necessary part of salvation. This was the motivation behind the covenant these leaders made. They had just recognized and confessed their sins as well as their consequences, and they wanted to change back to a people who loved and obeyed God. We will study this covenant more in the next chapter, but for now, we will take it as a fruit of repentance, a desire to turn from their wicked ways so they could live in peace with God and once again receive His blessings. Perhaps they remembered what God said to Solomon in 2 Chronicles 7:14: "If my people who are called by my name humble themselves, and pray and seek my face and turn from their wicked ways, then I will hear from heaven and will forgive their sin and heal their land."

How can we apply this subject of repentance to our businesses? Confession is incomplete without the desire to change and the belief that the power of God's Holy Spirit can and will change us. Just as surely as the Israelites in Nehemiah's day broke their covenant in Nehemiah chapter 13, so will you and I continue to sin, confess, and repent for the remainder of our lives. However, Scripture assures us that there will be progress. Therefore, as you take your faith to your business and practice prayerful repentance, your business will progress as well in its kingdom mission. This is not to say that repentance is the key to profitability. No, it is the key to becoming more like Christ, which will then take us closer to our kingdom goals.

In conclusion to our analysis of this prayer, what can we learn from these Nehemiah-led Israelites and God? First, be thankful and humble. Stay focused on God, and consider His mercy and blessing on your business. Stay hungry and focused on the mission of your kingdom business. Remember the vision God called you to. Next, face the facts that you and your team are going to sin. There is no way you or I are perfect. We are far from it. Be ready to confess and deal with sin. Encourage your people to be sin confessors and forgivers. Ask for big things in your prayers. If Israel could ask to be restored to God and for Him to rescue them from their oppressors, what can you and I ask for? Finally, as the apostle Paul says in Romans 12:2, "Be transformed by the renewal of your mind." Strive to continually repent by turning away from sin and toward Christ. We won't ever be perfect this side of heaven, but we can expect Him to do great things through us as we become more like Him.

View From the Trenches

It is one thing to be able to study and analyze Scripture, and understand the way things should be. It is quite another thing to be able to consistently apply Scripture to business or life. Busy Bees and its owners are no exception to this. In fact, at times, we have had enough sin at Busy Bees to fill our business as well as yours. The fact that we are a Christian school with Christian employees only means we are a bunch of saved sinners.

Despite this, we do try hard to utilize the various parts of this prayer in our day-to-day work. We thank God and praise Him in our Bible studies and team meetings, but we need to work on confession and repentance. As our teams have improved, these two items also have improved. Our employees don't seem to stay as angry at each other when there is conflict.

For me, I would say the area that has caused me to take my eyes off of God, even for a little while, is finances. Since finances are such a critical aspect of any business, as we have discussed, it is easy for me to spend my Busy Bees time focused almost exclusively on them. This was especially true when we were losing bucketfuls of money each month. There were times when I would be so stressed out about finances that I would not even think of Busy Bees in terms of what was being taught to the kids, or what type of spiritual impact I was having on the company. My mind was focused on cutting costs, adding more children, and paying off debt. I never went off the deep end and forgot God completely, but I do remember being at the point of despair several times and not praying for God's mercy and deliverance nearly enough. Studying Nehemiah and trying to emulate him has helped, but I have to confess that what has helped the most has been becoming profitable through God's grace. That might sound pretty crass, but there is no doubt that a tremendous amount of stress was relieved.

In terms of remembering God's mercy, it is extremely helpful to look back at how God placed the Busy Bees call in our hearts, how He put us in business, drew in customers, and helped us build our reputation and become a blessing to our customers. It is also amazing how He preserved us through some very, very rough times. Unknown to me until recently, there was a time when a group of employees, who no longer work at Busy Bees, would get drunk on the weekends and get into fistfights and all other types of mischief. Yet they would come to work Monday praising God's name, but also telling about all their wild weekend drunken exploits. It is incredible that God delivered us through such a mess in the name of Christ, and preserved our business despite the obvious sin that was happening at our school. In terms of identifying sin and rooting it out, we have become much better. First, our group of employees is far superior than it was, and second, we have become firmer at enforcing our expectations.

Regarding praying for "big things," we do ask God to help us expand our services so we can introduce Christ to thousands of children. That would be a gigantic leap, but we know He can do it.

For repentance, I know I need to be better at taking a genuine interest in my teams and customers. I can be more analytical in nature, as you can probably tell if you have read this far, and have a tendency to be more impatient with people than I should. Those are some key areas in which I need to change and become more Christlike.

Chapter 15

The People Make a Covenant With God: Nehemiah Chapter 10

But be doers of the word, and not hearers only, deceiving yourselves.

James 1:22

In Nehemiah chapter 9, we made general reference to the covenant the people made with God and examined it in terms of repentance. In Nehemiah chapter 10, the specifics of the covenant are discussed. Before we look at the particular aspects of this covenant and determine how to apply it to our businesses, let's take a step back and review where we have been.

We started with the Jewish nation in tatters, destitute and oppressed by the surrounding nations. They were unprotected physically, economically, and spiritually. One man with a heart for them, Nehemiah, dared to dream that God would use him to bring about their restoration. Because of his response to God's call, the people now had protection, a way of revitalizing their economy, and, most of all, their passion for God was restored. Now, as we look at the covenant, we will see what the leaders of the people believed were the chief tenets they believed were necessary to be faithful to God.

[1]"On the seals are the names of Nehemiah the governor, the son of Hacaliah, Zedekiah, [2]Seraiah, Azariah, Jeremiah, [3]Pashhur, Amariah, Malchijah, [4]Hattush, Shebaniah, Malluch, [5]Harim, Meremoth, Obadiah, [6]Daniel, Ginnethon, Baruch,

[7]Meshullam, Abijah, Mijamin, [8]Maaziah, Bilgai, Shemaiah; these are the priests. [9]And the Levites: Jeshua the son of Azaniah, Binnui of the sons of Henadad, Kadmiel; [10]and their brothers, Shebaniah, Hodiah, Kelita, Pelaiah, Hanan, [11]Mica, Rehob, Hashabiah, [12]Zaccur, Sherebiah, Shebaniah, [13]Hodiah, Bani, Beninu. [14]The chiefs of the people: Parosh, Pahath-moab, Elam, Zattu, Bani, [15]Bunni, Azgad, Bebai, [16]Adonijah, Bigvai, Adin, [17]Ater, Hezekiah, Azzur, [18]Hodiah, Hashum, Bezai, [19]Hariph, Anathoth, Nebai, [20]Magpiash, Meshullam, Hezir, [21]Meshezabel, Zadok, Jaddua, [22]Pelatiah, Hanan, Anaiah, [23]Hoshea, Hananiah, Hasshub, [24]Hallohesh, Pilha, Shobek, [25]Rehum, Hashabnah, Maaseiah, [26]Ahiah, Hanan, Anan, [27]Malluch, Harim, Baanah.

[28]"The rest of the people, the priests, the Levites, the gatekeepers, the singers, the temple servants, and all who have separated themselves from the peoples of the lands to the Law of God, their wives, their sons, their daughters, all who have knowledge and understanding, [29]join with their brothers, their nobles, and enter into a curse and an oath to walk in God's Law that was given by Moses the servant of God, and to observe and do all the commandments of the LORD our Lord and his rules and his statutes. [30]We will not give our daughters to the peoples of the land or take their daughters for our sons. [31]And if the peoples of the land bring in goods or any grain on the Sabbath day to sell, we will not buy from them on the Sabbath or on a holy day. And we will forego the crops of the seventh year and the exaction of every debt.

[32]"We also take on ourselves the obligation to give yearly a third part of a shekel for the service of the house of our God: [33]for the showbread, the regular grain offering, the regular burnt offering, the Sabbaths, the new moons, the appointed feasts, the holy things, and the sin offerings to make atonement for Israel, and for all the work of the house of our God. [34]We, the priests, the Levites, and the people, have likewise cast lots for the wood offering, to bring it into the house of our God, according to our fathers' houses, at

times appointed, year by year, to burn on the altar of the LORD our God, as it is written in the Law. [35]We obligate ourselves to bring the firstfruits of our ground and the firstfruits of all fruit of every tree, year by year, to the house of the LORD; [36]also to bring to the house of our God, to the priests who minister in the house of our God, the firstborn of our sons and of our cattle, as it is written in the Law, and the firstborn of our herds and of our flocks; [37]and to bring the first of our dough, and our contributions, the fruit of every tree, the wine and the oil, to the priests, to the chambers of the house of our God; and to bring to the Levites the tithes from our ground, for it is the Levites who collect the tithes in all our towns where we labor. [38]And the priest, the son of Aaron, shall be with the Levites when the Levites receive the tithes. And the Levites shall bring up the tithe of the tithes to the house of our God, to the chambers of the storehouse. [39]For the people of Israel and the sons of Levi shall bring the contribution of grain, wine, and oil to the chambers, where the vessels of the sanctuary are, as well as the priests who minister, and the gatekeepers and the singers. We will not neglect the house of our God."

The first thing to notice about this covenant was that it was widely accepted by the leaders as well as the common people. There was widespread agreement that this covenant would be the law of the land, that they would live by it in order to honor God and create the kind of culture that held Him in high regard. I believe this was their response to God's mercy toward them rather than an attempt to earn His grace and mercy. This is very similar to what the New Testament tells us our response should be toward Christ. Paul tells us in Romans and Galatians to walk by the Spirit, not by the flesh. Throughout his letters, the apostle gives us rules to live by, as does Jesus Himself. However, never is it mentioned that these rules save us. Rather, we are first saved and then respond to God out of gratitude by living in a way that is pleasing to Him.

Thinking about your business, I wonder if you have a set of rules, values, or principles that are known and accepted throughout your company as "what we believe in, what we do, and how we do it." I will share the Busy Bees core values statement later on in this chapter, but I mention the concept to you now because that is exactly what Nehemiah has laid out for us, a core values statement for the Israelites.

This covenant, or contract, with God had three main components. The first had to do with family; the second, with business; and the third, with church. Let's take a look at each of them and see how we can apply them to our businesses.

Family

First, in the family section, they promised not to let their sons and daughters intermarry with the pagan peoples around them. This is not because they were racists. Rather, this was a way to maintain the integrity of their faith. Intermarriage with people of other religions had been the downfall of the Jews throughout their history, despite God's many warnings against this practice. For some reason, probably our core sinful nature, even saved individuals tend to gravitate toward ungodliness when they are around it for extended periods of time. Solomon, with more than seven hundred wives from pagan nations, is a perfect example. This was the case over and over again when the Jewish people took spouses from other nations, and it is still the same today. Paul tells us in 2 Corinthians 6 not to be unequally yoked with unbelievers. This can apply to many circumstances, but especially in the most intimate of relationships—marriage.

How does this apply to our kingdom businesses? I believe this covenant recognizes the fact that we need to have God in all three main aspects of our lives—family first, business second, and church third. The Bible is filled with references to the importance of family and the nurturing effect we are to have on our children in teaching them about God. Scripture tells us our main responsibility is to take care of our families, to provide for them and teach them how to love God and live lives faithful to Him. In 1 Timothy chapter 3, Paul discusses the qualifications of elders in the church. One of the main ones is to have control of his family. The apostle says, "If someone does not know how to manage his own household, how will he care for God's church?" (v. 5). We can apply this same logic to a kingdom business. If you and I neglect or somehow fail to govern our families, for whatever reason, how can we realistically expect to successfully run a kingdom business? The argument is, If we cannot lead our families effectively, we have no right to be leading anything or anyone else.

I believe the placement of the family section of the covenant as number one is no accident. Without integrity and faithfulness at this core unit of society, the culture will crumble. The Jews proved it repeatedly, and modern society is repeating it as well. If you are a parent or grandparent, know someone who has children, or plan to have children at some point in your life, here are some things Scripture teaches us:

Deuteronomy 6:4-9:

Hear, O Israel: The LORD our God, the LORD is one. You shall love the LORD your God with all your heart and with all your soul and with all your might. And these words that I command you today shall be on your heart. You shall teach them diligently to your children, and shall talk of them when you sit in your house, and when you walk by the way, and when you lie down, and when you rise. You shall bind them as a sign on your hand, and they shall be as frontlets between your eyes. You shall write them on the doorposts of your house and on your gates.

We are commanded to integrate scriptural teachings into all aspects of our relationships with our children. As parents, we are the main disciplers of our kids. This is the primary means by which the gospel will be passed down to them. Of course, these verses assume we understand the Scriptures ourselves and are able to teach and model them to our children.

Proverbs 22:6:

Train up a child in the way he should go; even when he is old he will not depart from it.

Similar to the Deuteronomy passage, this verse assumes we know how to train and model the Scriptures to our kids, and commands us to do so. From listening to pastors teach this verse over the years, I have come to understand it to be what is referred to as a "truism," as opposed to a hard and fast promise. That means if we do what this verse says, most of the time, our kids are going to embrace the Lord. That is better than a minority of the time if we do not teach them the Scriptures.

Clearly, God places tremendous responsibility on Christian parents, but please do not think you are excluded if you are a grandparent, youth worker, Sunday school teacher, athletic coach, music instructor, aunt, uncle, or single friend to someone with children. We as a community of believers have the responsibility to come alongside parents and help them nurture and teach their children in the ways of God. If we neglect this responsibility, our children will not know right from wrong and will not know basic principles, such as, "Do not be unequally yoked with unbelievers," which is found in this covenant. Consider the following heart-wrenching verses from Judges 2:7-10.

> And the people served the LORD all the days of Joshua, and all the days of the elders who outlived Joshua, who had seen all the great work that the LORD had done for Israel. And Joshua the son of Nun, the servant of the LORD, died at the age of 110 years. And they buried him within the boundaries of his inheritance in Timnath-heres, in the hill country of Ephraim, north of the mountain of Gaash. And all that generation also were gathered to their fathers. And there arose another generation after them who did not know the LORD or the work that he had done for Israel.

They begin the pattern of decline for Israel after having conquered the Promised Land under the leadership of Joshua. If you read between the lines and consider how such a decline could have been possible, two things come to mind: one, not having a leader to replace Joshua; and two, parents failing to train their children as well as themselves in the ways of the Lord. We are only a generation away from turning our backs on God, as these verses show. Please do your best to ensure it does not occur in your household.

Now, before you go on a guilt trip about your failings as a parent, let me remind you that you are not, have never been, and never will be a perfect parent. We already read 1 John, which told us we are sinners. Nevertheless, we do have the Holy Spirit working in us to make us more like Christ each day. I just want us all to agree that raising our kids in the Lord is more important than having a great business. Fortunately, they are not mutually exclusive; otherwise, the second part of the covenant, dealing with business practices, would not be included.

Business Practices

Starting in verse 31, the covenant made with God by the people deals with business practices. It specifically says they will not do business on the Sabbath day and that every seventh year, they will leave their land fallow and cancel all debts. These particular principles come out of the commandments in Exodus 20, Deuteronomy 15, and Leviticus 25. Some argue whether or not the Sabbath still needs to be kept, and others argue whether the Old Testament civil law governing ancient Israel still needs to be kept. I hate to disappoint you, but we are not going to attempt to resolve those arguments here. Instead, just like we did with the first part of the covenant regarding families, we are going to use these as a springboard to build a framework for thinking about our businesses. Since we have covered much territory with the main premise of this book, using scriptural principles to create a kingdom business, we will not be repetitious. However, there are a few general principles worth pondering.

First, consider the radical concepts involved in these two principles—only doing business six days a week, and forgiving debts every seven years. Granted, the part of debt forgiveness must be read in its proper context. That notwithstanding, both are radical concepts under any circumstances. Businesses tend to be open on Sundays in America. Why? Business owners are afraid of losing opportunities for sales. What if they decided to do what God decided to do on the seventh day, rest? What if we worshiped and rested instead of following the ways of the world? My guess is God would honor that.

The point is, these people used principles from Scripture and incorporated them into their businesses. I cannot state this forcefully enough. We do not need to follow the practices of the world in our businesses. They lead to destruction, not prosperity. We need to be radically different. I have pointed you back to Romans many times during this book, and I do so again to point out the radical difference between the Christian and nonbeliever. Hear these verses from the apostle in Romans 8:5-8:

> For those who live according to the flesh set their minds on the things of the flesh, but those who live according to the Spirit set their minds on the things of the Spirit. For to set the mind on the flesh is death, but to set the mind on the Spirit is life and peace. For the mind that is set on the flesh is hostile to God, for it does not submit to God's law; indeed, it cannot. Those who are in the flesh cannot please God.

Do you see what the apostle is saying here? The sinful mind is hostile to God. In its hostility, it also develops business practices that are hostile to God. The mind of the Christian desires to live according to the laws of the Holy Spirit and have his mind set on what He desires. For the Christian business owner, that means we build scripturally based business practices that please God the Holy Spirit. That is the direction in which our minds are being led by Him. In contrast, the mind of the non-Christian business owner is going in the opposite direction in stark contrast to what God wants. Previously, I spoke to you about reading literature written by non-Christian business authors, or at least written by those who take a neutral stand. I do not pretend to judge the heart of any writer. Much of what is written is brilliant and spectacularly helpful. I personally have a large library of it and plan to continue buying and reading it. However, we must always, always, always read it critically and run it through the filter of Scripture.

Most of all, I encourage you not to fear creating explicitly Christian business practices. Returning to Romans 8:15, Paul tells us "⁵For you did not receive the spirit of slavery to fall back into fear, but you have received the Spirit of adoption as sons." We are Christ's. First Corinthians chapter 2 even says we have the mind of Christ. Do not fear that your business will not be profitable, that you will be ostracized, or that you will lose market share as a result of following Christian principles. If you find yourself in doubt and fear, read Psalm 37 over and over again, as I do. Can you imagine any more reassuring words than the following (vv. 1-8) from that psalm?

Fret not yourself because of evildoers;
be not envious of wrongdoers!
For they will soon fade like the grass
and wither like the green herb.

Trust in the LORD, and do good;
dwell in the land and befriend faithfulness.
Delight yourself in the LORD,
and he will give you the desires of your heart.

Commit your way to the LORD;
trust in him, and he will act.
He will bring forth your righteousness as the light,
and your justice as the noonday.

Be still before the LORD and wait patiently for him;
fret not yourself over the one who prospers in his way,
over the man who carries out evil devices!

Refrain from anger, and forsake wrath!
Fret not yourself; it tends only to evil.

Now, let's proceed to the third part of the covenant, church attendance and service. Fellow entrepreneur and business leader, it is difficult not to follow the world, and we often feel like we will be missing out by doing so. I hope through these verses, you see that just the opposite is true.

Church

The third and longest part of the covenant deals with the relationship of the people to the church. As you read verses 32-39, you will see that the people promised to make sacrifices of money, time, and crops. All of it is summarized in the words "We will not neglect the house of our God."

Before we get into the particulars, it is important to note that church attendance was expected of these people, and God expects us to worship Him together as well. The writer to the Hebrews summarizes this in chapter 10, verse 25 by telling us to not "[neglect] to meet together, as is the habit of some, but [encourage] one another, and all the more as you see the Day drawing near."

In a time when church attendance has declined in many parts of America and Europe, it is time for you and me as kingdom business owners to stand up and serve the church. We cannot truly be effective as kingdom business builders if we are not also committed to building God's kingdom by attending a church and participating in its life.

Moving on, let's deal with why this is listed as the third element of the covenant. I hope it is fairly obvious. I believe what the order of the covenant implies is that people should have their own lives ordered in accordance with God's commands in order for their sacrifice and service to the church to really be effective and pleasing to God. God considers His church holy, the bride of Christ. It is supposed to be pure and spotless by the blood of Christ. Therefore, God sets high standards for it and will do whatever He deems necessary to protect it. None of this is to say we have to have our lives perfectly in order before we can be of any use to the church. It says we need to consistently apply the Scriptures to our entire lives, not just on Sundays. We are to look at and live our lives as though everything in them is under the authority of Scripture, not just church. Everything in our lives needs to fall under the dominion of Jesus Christ. The consistency of applying Scripture to our families and businesses makes us even more effective when we serve in and sacrifice for the church.

One of the striking aspects of this passage is that of bringing money and the fruit of our labor to the church. This passage of

Scripture has prescribed amounts per family. Today there are no prescribed amounts, except for the tithe, but I encourage you to read 1 Corinthians chapter 16 and 2 Corinthians chapters 8 and 9 to hear what the apostle Paul has to say about offerings. Traditionally, the tithe has been 10 percent of the "firstfruits." It seems to me that means gross earnings as we would typically understand it today. However you interpret it, I strongly encourage you to pray about what God would have you give to the church financially, not only as a tithe, but also in offerings for foreign missions, ministries to the poor, or whatever else your church supports. Remember, one of the reasons you have a kingdom business is this very purpose. If God blesses your business, you will have far more to give than most other people. Through a successful and prosperous business, you have the opportunity to build a new sanctuary for your church, pay off its debt, purchase land for a new one, provide support for multiple missionaries, or whatever else God puts on your heart. Just remember, this is what your business is all about, not the accumulation of wealth simply to keep it for yourself. The following passage from 2 Corinthians 9:10-14 gives us a wonderful insight into God's purpose for wealth:

> He who supplies seed to the sower and bread for food will supply and multiply your seed for sowing and increase the harvest of your righteousness. You will be enriched in every way to be generous in every way, which through us will produce thanksgiving to God. For the ministry of this service is not only supplying the needs of the saints but is also over-flowing in many thanksgivings to God. By their approval of this service, they will glorify God because of your submission flowing from your confession of the gospel of Christ, and the generosity of your contribution for them and for all others, while they long for you and pray for you, because of the surpassing grace of God upon you.

The wealth you and your kingdom business create comes from God, and He has given it to you so that you can be generous on every occasion and supply the needs of God's people. As a result of your generosity, thanksgiving and praise will be made to God. That is an awesome legacy.

The next part of the passage speaks of each family bringing wood for the burnt offerings at appointed times of the year. Let's take this a step further and call it service to the church. Do you realize that the 80/20 principle discussed earlier also applies to church service? That is, 80 percent of the work is done by 20 percent of the people. Many people in our churches come for Sunday services and have nothing at all to do with the church or any of its members the rest of the week. While it is good they are there to hear the Word, they are depriving the church not only of their gifts, but also of their fellowship and encouragement. There are so many needs in any given church, and I encourage you to be one of those committed and energetic people who make it a priority to serve in some capacity, whether serving in children's ministries, having people into your home for meals, serving the elderly, or taking on an official position like deacon or elder.

One thing is for sure: The church needs people with your gifts and experience. Consider all the experience you have as a business leader. You are a planner, a strategist, a tactician, a project manager, a raiser of capital, a reader of financial statements, a teacher and discipler of people, and much more. How can the church not benefit from your skills and experience? I think you will find there is much need for what you, as a kingdom businessperson, can bring to your church. Please do not be shy about using your gifts.

One last point to make about the service in the church from these verses is that it was done by families. For those of you with children, and even for those without, note the impact of having children serve in the church from a very young age, even if it is "just" carrying wood, as verse 34 mentions. Sometimes we neglect to even consider the fact that our children can and should serve in the church. By watching you, they will have a good role model who shows them service in the church is just a normal part of life. I encourage you to actively think of ways your children can serve in the church as well. They can pass out bulletins, help greet visitors, set up and take down chairs and tables for fellowship dinners, work in the nursery, and help clean up after Sunday services, just to name a few.

I hope the study of this covenant has been instructive to you. While we cannot expect to keep God's laws perfectly, the covenant these people made coming out of a desire to repent of their sins and turn their lives toward God is a model for all of us. The key elements of family, business, and church show us that every aspect of our lives should be ordered by Scripture, culminating in a strong and thriving church community that gives glory to God as a witness in its community.

View From the Trenches: Family

Regarding our family, nothing is more important to Cindy and me than our two children, Andrew and Emilia, coming to salvation in Christ and growing into productive members of the church and society. Certainly, this is in the Lord's hands, and we are daily faced with our own failings as parents. Nevertheless, we press on in prayer and within the framework of family worship several times a week, church, and homeschooling.

Just a quick note on homeschooling. No doubt, many of you reading this book have sent your children to government-sponsored schools. Cindy and I are products of those schools, as are all our friends and parents. We consider ourselves fairly well-educated, but we learned nothing compared to the wonderful education our children are receiving through homeschooling. The ability home-schoolers have to probe subjects deeply through a Christian world-view and life view is truly astonishing. While there are many fine teachers, parents, and administrators involved with the government schools, in America, the expression of a Christian worldview and life view is largely prohibited, while views that are expressly anti-Christian are not only tolerated, but encouraged. We choose not to expose our children to this environment, where the creation is worshiped, rather than the Creator. Having said this, we have fine Christian friends who have their children in government schools. That is their right and choice, and we have no right to judge them. We simply chose not to go that route with our children.

As all of you with children understand, giving them your time is the most important thing you can do for them. It is also one of the most challenging things for driven entrepreneurs. I try to remind myself that the years tick away rapidly, and make sure we spend a lot of time together as a family.

Within the framework of spending time together, education, and modeling, we are trying to gradually introduce our children to our businesses. Our deep desire is that in owning businesses, we can show our children that there is an excellent alternative to working for someone else. They can own their own business just like their parents. While they are certainly free to pursue whatever avenues they choose, we definitely want them to have exposure to entrepreneurial thinking and activity at early ages.

View From the Trenches: Business

Earlier in this chapter, I mentioned having a set of core values. I will attach the Busy Bees core values below. Being an expressly Christian school is certainly an enormous and refreshing contrast to any place I have ever worked. We have many platforms we use to teach the gospel to students, parents, and our staff. Besides our classroom teaching, we make judicious use of emails to parents through *Infusion*, our monthly newsletter, and various programs and open houses throughout the year. We can even be explicitly Christian in our advertising. We just figure people will come if they are interested, and so far we seem to be drawing a crowd by God's grace. Here are our core values as I delivered to our employees:

Things We Live and Breathe by at
Busy Bees Christian PreSchool

1. Jesus Christ is our King, and Busy Bees exists to bring glory to Him. Helping the children we serve come to salvation in Christ is why we exist.

2. Each Busy Bees team member is an ambassador of Christ and should conduct himself or herself accordingly. We might be the only exposure our families and children get to the gospel. Helping our team members grow in their relationships with Christ is important to us.

3. We depend on referrals, and those are dependent upon us delivering customer service that goes far beyond what they expect and what is delivered by other preschools and day cares. We need to consistently create "Wow!" experiences for our customers. We should approach each encounter with a customer as an opportunity to solve a problem, share a concern, and go the extra mile.

4. Innovation is expected at Busy Bees. We all should constantly be thinking about how to make the experience better for our customers.

5. Busy Bees will be led and managed by responsible business principles that satisfy the needs of customers and employees while providing a profit for the owners.

6. We are a team of early childhood education specialists, and we strive to bring the best and most appropriate teaching methods to our school while conducting ourselves as professionals each day. Helping each other get the job done is what we do.

7. We are in the people development business, and the growth and development of our team members are important to us. Management will strive to create fair policies that attract the best people, give them challenging assignments, and reward them for outstanding performance.

8. The safety of the children we serve is of utmost importance. We will develop, train, and adhere to policies that ensure safety.

9. Prayer is our most powerful weapon and should be an integral part of Busy Bees. Pray for each other as well as the children and families we serve.

10. Open communication is key, and employees are encouraged to share concerns with management. Likewise, management will strive to openly communicate decisions and policies with employees and customers in a consistent and timely manner. Communication should occur in a spirit of love, humility, and respect.

View From the Trenches: Church

I have already told you a little about our church life. Church is a huge part of our lives. Rather than going into our various activities, I just want to reiterate that Christianity is a "team sport," so to speak. It is where God's people come together in an extremely powerful way. He designed it so we can teach and encourage one another, have fellowship, and help spread the gospel using the various gifts He has given us. If you are not active in a vibrant church body, I encourage you in the strongest terms to find a Bible-believing evangelical church where you can serve and grow in your faith alongside other believers. While we have spent much time examining Nehemiah and the power of individuals within this book, Nehemiah's energy was directed essentially to what was then the church, Israel. So while your kingdom business is extremely important to the cause of the King, its purpose is to help build the church.

Chapter 16

The Kingdom People Move Into the New City: Nehemiah Chapter 11

You are the light of the world. A city set on a hill cannot be hidden.

Matthew 5:14

In the previous chapter, we focused on the relationship of you and your kingdom business to the church, and we will expand on that thought in Nehemiah chapter 11. As I encouraged you in the last chapter to be a strong participant in your church, in this chapter, I want to encourage you to be an advocate of church attendance and service to your customers, vendors, and employees. In order to develop this point more fully, let's read Nehemiah chapter 11.

¹Now the leaders of the people lived in Jerusalem. And the rest of the people cast lots to bring one out of ten to live in Jerusalem the holy city, while nine out of ten remained in the other towns. ²And the people blessed all the men who willingly offered to live in Jerusalem.

³These are the chiefs of the province who lived in Jerusalem; but in the towns of Judah everyone lived on his property in their towns: Israel, the priests, the Levites, the temple servants, and the descendants of Solomon's servants. ⁴And in Jerusalem lived certain of the sons of Judah and of the

sons of Benjamin. Of the sons of Judah: Athaiah the son of Uzziah, son of Zechariah, son of Amariah, son of Shephatiah, son of Mahalalel, of the sons of Perez; [5]and Maaseiah the son of Baruch, son of Col-hozeh, son of Hazaiah, son of Adaiah, son of Joiarib, son of Zechariah, son of the Shilonite. [6]All the sons of Perez who lived in Jerusalem were 468 valiant men.

[7]And these are the sons of Benjamin: Sallu the son of Meshullam, son of Joed, son of Pedaiah, son of Kolaiah, son of Maaseiah, son of Ithiel, son of Jeshaiah, [8]and his brothers, men of valor, 928. [9]Joel the son of Zichri was their overseer; and Judah the son of Hassenuah was second over the city.

[10]Of the priests: Jedaiah the son of Joiarib, Jachin, [11]Seraiah the son of Hilkiah, son of Meshullam, son of Zadok, son of Meraioth, son of Ahitub, ruler of the house of God, [12]and their brothers who did the work of the house, 822; and Adaiah the son of Jeroham, son of Pelaliah, son of Amzi, son of Zechariah, son of Pashhur, son of Malchijah, [13]and his brothers, heads of fathers' houses, 242; and Amashsai, the son of Azarel, son of Ahzai, son of Meshillemoth, son of Immer, [14]and their brothers, mighty men of valor, 128; their overseer was Zabdiel the son of Haggedolim.

[15]And of the Levites: Shemaiah the son of Hasshub, son of Azrikam, son of Hashabiah, son of Bunni; [16]and Shabbethai and Jozabad, of the chiefs of the Levites, who were over the outside work of the house of God; [17]and Mattaniah the son of Mica, son of Zabdi, son of Asaph, who was the leader of the praise, who gave thanks, and Bakbukiah, the second among his brothers; and Abda the son of Shammua, son of Galal, son of Jeduthun. [18]All the Levites in the holy city were 284.

[19]The gatekeepers, Akkub, Talmon and their brothers, who kept watch at the gates, were 172. [20]And the rest of Israel, and of the priests and the Levites, were in all the towns of Judah, every one in his inheritance. [21]But the temple servants lived on Ophel; and Ziha and Gishpa were over the temple servants.

[22]The overseer of the Levites in Jerusalem was Uzzi the son of Bani, son of Hashabiah, son of Mattaniah, son of

Mica, of the sons of Asaph, the singers, over the work of the house of God. [23]For there was a command from the king concerning them, and a fixed provision for the singers, as every day required. [24]And Pethahiah the son of Meshezabel, of the sons of Zerah the son of Judah, was at the king's side in all matters concerning the people.

[25]And as for the villages, with their fields, some of the people of Judah lived in Kiriath-arba and its villages, and in Dibon and its villages, and in Jekabzeel and its villages, [26]and in Jeshua and in Moladah and Beth-pelet, [27]in Hazar-shual, in Beersheba and its villages, [28]in Ziklag, in Meconah and its villages, [29]in En-rimmon, in Zorah, in Jarmuth, [30]Zanoah, Adullam, and their villages, Lachish and its fields, and Azekah and its villages. So they encamped from Beersheba to the Valley of Hinnom. [31]The people of Benjamin also lived from Geba onward, at Michmash, Aija, Bethel and its villages, [32]Anathoth, Nob, Ananiah, [33]Hazor, Ramah, Gittaim, [34]Hadid, Zeboim, Neballat, [35]Lod, and Ono, the valley of craftsmen. [36]And certain divisions of the Levites in Judah were assigned to Benjamin.

With all the effort made to rebuild the city and its walls, it may come as a surprise to you that only 10 percent of the population was able to live in the city. The remaining 90 percent had to live in the countryside in their own towns. The city simply was not big enough to hold the entire population. If this was the case, what was the point of this entire endeavor? Why make such a massive effort to build something that could only house 10 percent of the population? I believe the answer goes back to what I have been saying about the church.

While not all the Israelites could live in the city of Jerusalem, having it rebuilt strengthened and unified them culturally, economically, politically, and spiritually. This was Nehemiah's intent when he began the work. He knew God's people needed to be unified on many fronts, or they would continue in their downward spiral into poverty, misery, and oppression to other nations. So we see the wisdom of Nehemiah. He knew that his ultimate purpose was not to build a wall. Rather, his true mission was to help build God's church. That, my friends, is your purpose, too.

Symbolically, it seems to me that Jerusalem in this chapter represents the church, the unifying spiritual force for God's people. The 10 percent who lived there seem to be made up of leaders and other church officials and workers such as priests and Levites. This is where the temple was located, where the people came to worship, serve, and make their sacrifices.

The 90 percent of the people who lived in the countryside in their own towns and villages represents you and me as well as all believers out in the world making a living. The kingdom work is being done daily, not just in the church, but in the outlying towns as well, represented by our kingdom businesses. But what is the goal of the kingdom business? What is the unifying spiritual force behind the kingdom business? Of course, it is the church. While we serve customers, produce products, and train employees for the glory of God, our ultimate purpose is to build the body of believers through God's church. That has been the theme of this book as we have explored Nehemiah, and I hope you embrace it as the primary purpose behind your business. While it is true that through our businesses we are meant to symbolically be the light of the world and a city set on a hill, this verse really pertains to the church. God's church is meant to stand apart as a beacon of hope in a dark and cruel world, and it is our job, as entrepreneurs, to help it shine brightly.

If you have a small business, I hope you do not feel it is too small to make an impact on the church. God has a history of using small groups of people in extremely mighty ways. Consider Gideon's small army of three hundred men and the massive victory God gave them over a mighty enemy.

Look also at the relatively small group of apostles and their followers, who were accused of "turning the world upside down" in Acts chapter 17. If you have a small business, do not underestimate His ability to use you in ways you cannot possibly imagine, just as He has used small groups of people throughout history to make great contributions for His kingdom. How big was Nehemiah's "business" when he started? Yet, look at how he was used by God. In this regard, I encourage you to continually think beyond yourself.

To whom can you train the principles of kingdom entrepreneurship and business leadership so they can build businesses to do the same thing? If you constantly think of replication like the apostles and early church did, I believe you can have an impact that is unimaginable. If you doubt me, take another look at Ephesians 3:20-21: "Now to him who is able to do far more abundantly than all that we ask or think, according to the power at work within us, to him be glory in the church and in Christ Jesus throughout all generations, forever and ever. Amen."

View From the Trenches

I have to admit that I am convicted as I write these words, specifically from the standpoint of not making more information on local churches available to our Busy Bees customers. I have been so focused on building the business that I have neglected one of the main purposes for our establishment. Sure, our customers can go find a church on their own, but many of them do not come from a Christian background, and others do not make the time for church. For several years, I have been thinking about having a church literature rack in our lobby, and now I am intent on getting this done.

This brings up an important point for you to consider: Your kingdom business will be as close to a church as many of your customers ever get. What can you do in your business to promote local churches specifically, and the importance of church attendance and membership in general? As a beacon, your light should lead people to Christ and the church. How can you modify your operation to facilitate this?

Chapter 17

The Kingdom People Celebrate God's Goodness: Nehemiah Chapter 12

And I heard every creature in heaven and on earth and under the earth and in the sea, and all that is in them, saying, "To him who sits on the throne and to the Lamb be blessing and honor and glory and might forever and ever!"

Revelation 5:13

Have you ever heard of someone having a spiritual "mountaintop experience"? If there ever was one, it is witnessed here in chapter 12 of Nehemiah. The wall was complete, Jerusalem was a functioning, worshiping city inhabited by 10 percent of the population, and the people were reunified in their desire to worship and serve God. Now they were ready for a great celebration of praise and worship to God for the wonderful things He had done for them. Let's read chapter 12 and get a glimpse of this remarkable worship service.

¹These are the priests and the Levites who came up with Zerubbabel the son of Shealtiel, and Jeshua: Seraiah, Jeremiah, Ezra, ²Amariah, Malluch, Hattush, ³Shecaniah, Rehum, Meremoth, ⁴Iddo, Ginnethoi, Abijah, ⁵Mijamin, Maadiah, Bilgah, ⁶Shemaiah, Joiarib, Jedaiah, ⁷Sallu, Amok,

Hilkiah, Jedaiah. These were the chiefs of the priests and of their brothers in the days of Jeshua.

[8]And the Levites: Jeshua, Binnui, Kadmiel, Sherebiah, Judah, and Mattaniah, who with his brothers was in charge of the songs of thanksgiving. [9]And Bakbukiah and Unni and their brothers stood opposite them in the service. [10]And Jeshua was the father of Joiakim, Joiakim the father of Eliashib, Eliashib the father of Joiada, [11]Joiada the father of Jonathan, and Jonathan the father of Jaddua.

[12]And in the days of Joiakim were priests, heads of fathers' houses: of Seraiah, Meraiah; of Jeremiah, Hananiah; [13]of Ezra, Meshullam; of Amariah, Jehohanan; [14]of Malluchi, Jonathan; of Shebaniah, Joseph; [15]of Harim, Adna; of Meraioth, Helkai; [16]of Iddo, Zechariah; of Ginnethon, Meshullam; [17]of Abijah, Zichri; of Miniamin, of Moadiah, Piltai; [18]of Bilgah, Shammua; of Shemaiah, Jehonathan; [19]of Joiarib, Mattenai; of Jedaiah, Uzzi; [20]of Sallai, Kallai; of Amok, Eber; [21]of Hilkiah, Hashabiah; of Jedaiah, Nethanel.

[22]In the days of Eliashib, Joiada, Johanan, and Jaddua, the Levites were recorded as heads of fathers' houses; so too were the priests in the reign of Darius the Persian. [23]As for the sons of Levi, their heads of fathers' houses were written in the Book of the Chronicles until the days of Johanan the son of Eliashib. [24]And the chiefs of the Levites: Hashabiah, Sherebiah, and Jeshua the son of Kadmiel, with their brothers who stood opposite them, to praise and to give thanks, according to the commandment of David the man of God, watch by watch. [25]Mattaniah, Bakbukiah, Obadiah, Meshullam, Talmon, and Akkub were gatekeepers standing guard at the storehouses of the gates. [26]These were in the days of Joiakim the son of Jeshua son of Jozadak, and in the days of Nehemiah the governor and of Ezra, the priest and scribe.

[27]And at the dedication of the wall of Jerusalem they sought the Levites in all their places, to bring them to Jerusalem to celebrate the dedication with gladness, with thanksgivings and with singing, with cymbals, harps, and

lyres. [28]And the sons of the singers gathered together from the district surrounding Jerusalem and from the villages of the Netophathites; [29]also from Beth-gilgal and from the region of Geba and Azmaveth, for the singers had built for themselves villages around Jerusalem. [30]And the priests and the Levites purified themselves, and they purified the people and the gates and the wall.

[31]Then I brought the leaders of Judah up onto the wall and appointed two great choirs that gave thanks. One went to the south on the wall to the Dung Gate. [32]And after them went Hoshaiah and half of the leaders of Judah, [33]and Azariah, Ezra, Meshullam, [34]Judah, Benjamin, Shemaiah, and Jeremiah, [35]and certain of the priests' sons with trumpets: Zechariah the son of Jonathan, son of Shemaiah, son of Mattaniah, son of Micaiah, son of Zaccur, son of Asaph; [36]and his relatives, Shemaiah, Azarel, Milalai, Gilalai, Maai, Nethanel, Judah, and Hanani, with the musical instruments of David the man of God. And Ezra the scribe went before them. [37]At the Fountain Gate they went up straight before them by the stairs of the city of David, at the ascent of the wall, above the house of David, to the Water Gate on the east.

[38]The other choir of those who gave thanks went to the north, and I followed them with half of the people, on the wall, above the Tower of the Ovens, to the Broad Wall, [39]and above the Gate of Ephraim, and by the Gate of Yeshanah, and by the Fish Gate and the Tower of Hananel and the Tower of the Hundred, to the Sheep Gate; and they came to a halt at the Gate of the Guard. [40]So both choirs of those who gave thanks stood in the house of God, and I and half of the officials with me; [41]and the priests Eliakim, Maaseiah, Miniamin, Micaiah, Elioenai, Zechariah, and Hananiah, with trumpets; [42]and Maaseiah, Shemaiah, Eleazar, Uzzi, Jehohanan, Malchijah, Elam, and Ezer. And the singers sang with Jezrahiah as their leader. [43]And they offered great sacrifices that day and rejoiced, for God had made them rejoice

with great joy; the women and children also rejoiced. And the joy of Jerusalem was heard far away.

[44]On that day men were appointed over the storerooms, the contributions, the firstfruits, and the tithes, to gather into them the portions required by the Law for the priests and for the Levites according to the fields of the towns, for Judah rejoiced over the priests and the Levites who ministered. [45]And they performed the service of their God and the service of purification, as did the singers and the gatekeepers, according to the command of David and his son Solomon. [46]For long ago in the days of David and Asaph there were directors of the singers, and there were songs of praise and thanksgiving to God. [47]And all Israel in the days of Zerubbabel and in the days of Nehemiah gave the daily portions for the singers and the gatekeepers; and they set apart that which was for the Levites; and the Levites set apart that which was for the sons of Aaron.

I would definitely like to have been at this worship service. With this long list of priests, Levites, gatekeepers, singers, musicians, and leaders of Judah, it must have been quite a site. There were two great choirs on top of the wall, facing each other, possibly even responding to each other. There were trumpets and other musical instruments, such as cymbals, harps, and lyres. Some of the priests offered sacrifices to God. There was great singing and rejoicing by the entire population, and the sound of singing and rejoicing could be heard far outside the city.

What was going on here? They were celebrating God's incredible mercy toward them. Remember the prayer back in Nehemiah chapter 9 in which the people mentioned God's repeated acts of mercy and kindness toward the continually sinful and ungrateful people? Well, here Israel was again, rejoicing at God's grace toward them. They had done nothing to deserve His mercy, but true to His promise, He had chastised them for a while through the Babylonian captivity, and now He had brought them completely back as a people and culture. He had led them from ruins into worship, discipleship, repentance, blessing, and now great rejoicing. With examples like this, can we ever be in doubt of God's faithfulness?

It is no surprise to God that we are inconsistent in our faith and frequently unfaithful to Him. He is used to it. It has been part of the historical record for thousands of years. So what does He do about it? Romans 5:8 tells us what He does and gives us just as much reason to rejoice as these Israelites. It says, "But God shows His love for us in that while we were still sinners, Christ died for us."

Amazingly, God sent Christ to die for us and bring us into His kingdom while we were still sinners and His enemies. That is great cause for rejoicing each time we worship together. Have you really thought about that and how it applies to worship? Looking at this worship service in Nehemiah, and then considering what Christ did for us, can we ever justify having a dull, boring, lifeless worship service where we go through the motions and can't wait to get out the door? It really is inconceivable that such a thing could occur based on the great salvation that has accrued to us through Christ. Every time we worship together, we should be celebrating our deliverance from hell and our entry into God's eternal family, where we have unimaginable blessings. If you think I am crazy and making too big of a deal out of this, go back to the beginning of this chapter and reread the Scripture from Revelation, which is a scene right out of heaven. In fact, read Revelation chapter 5 to gain insight into the kind of loud praise and worship that will occur in heaven. The worship service in Nehemiah chapter 12 reminds me of the joyful worship of Christ in Revelation and should remind us of the grateful praise we should be bringing to God each week.

Notice in this worship service who was not praised . . . Nehemiah! But he was the man who made it all possible, right? Without his heart of compassion for God's people and his faithful and tenacious follow-through, none of His people would have been there, right? Surely, he was due a little credit! Not really. Nehemiah and everyone else knew that what had happened was a team effort guided and blessed by God. Nehemiah was a humble leader, just as you and I need to be humble leaders in our businesses and churches. It is not about us, especially for kingdom entrepreneurs. It is all about giving glory to God and building His church, which is what we see happening here.

After the worship service, we read about some of the duties of the people who worked full time in the church, such as priests, Levites, singers, and gatekeepers. We see that all Israel contributed to their livelihood and that they were pleased with their ministering priests and Levites. This brings us back to a familiar theme, which is how your kingdom business impacts the church. Do you realize that without the contributions of your business and others like it, ministers can't minister, singers can't sing, and God's church can't survive and grow? People like you and me with kingdom businesses directly impact the ability of the church to carry out its ministries. In fact, by God's grace, as wealth builders and acquirers of capital, we have the ability to enable many people to worship and praise God, not just at our own church, but throughout the world by supporting world missions and church plants right here in America.

Finally, I encourage you to show appreciation for those who minster in God's church, not just monetarily, but through encouragement and friendship as well. Being a pastor is a demanding job, and they need our prayers and support just as much as we need theirs. What have you done for your pastor lately? How can you encourage him and help share his load?

View From the Trenches

One of the great blessings our businesses have allowed us to accomplish is strong support of world missions through our church. As our church has raised support each year for this cause, Cindy and I have been able to meet and befriend many great missionaries as they have visited our church over the years, and through our entrepreneurial activities, God has enabled us to make very significant contributions to their support. It is a great feeling to know that God has used part of the fruit of our risk-taking and labor to send people all around the world to preach the gospel, start new churches, and help people with their medical needs.

Chapter 18

The Kingdom People Return to Their Old Ways: Nehemiah Chapter 13

And they came to Jerusalem. And he entered the temple and began to drive out those who sold and those who bought in the temple, and he overturned the tables of the money-changers and the seats of those who sold pigeons.

Mark 11:15

If only the book of Nehemiah had ended with the marvelous worship service in Nehemiah chapter 12. But "mountaintop experiences" tend to be short-lived, and real life soon overwhelms us. As we look at the final chapter of Nehemiah, we see ourselves trying to make a difference in a corrupt culture. We are shown the need for each of us to maintain our leadership and vision with great diligence and passion, and underlying it all, we see the overarching need to replicate ourselves with similarly passionate leaders. Here is the final chapter of Nehemiah:

¹On that day they read from the Book of Moses in the hearing of the people. And in it was found written that no Ammonite or Moabite should ever enter the assembly of God, ²for they did not meet the people of Israel with bread and water, but hired Balaam against them to curse them— yet our God turned the curse into a blessing. ³As soon as the

people heard the law, they separated from Israel all those of foreign descent.

⁴Now before this, Eliashib the priest, who was appointed over the chambers of the house of our God, and who was related to Tobiah, ⁵prepared for Tobiah a large chamber where they had previously put the grain offering, the frankincense, the vessels, and the tithes of grain, wine, and oil, which were given by commandment to the Levites, singers, and gatekeepers, and the contributions for the priests. ⁶While this was taking place, I was not in Jerusalem, for in the thirty-second year of Artaxerxes king of Babylon I went to the king. And after some time I asked leave of the king ⁷and came to Jerusalem, and I then discovered the evil that Eliashib had done for Tobiah, preparing for him a chamber in the courts of the house of God. ⁸And I was very angry, and I threw all the household furniture of Tobiah out of the chamber. ⁹Then I gave orders, and they cleansed the chambers, and I brought back there the vessels of the house of God, with the grain offering and the frankincense.

¹⁰I also found out that the portions of the Levites had not been given to them, so that the Levites and the singers, who did the work, had fled each to his field. ¹¹So I confronted the officials and said, "Why is the house of God forsaken?" And I gathered them together and set them in their stations. ¹²Then all Judah brought the tithe of the grain, wine, and oil into the storehouses. ¹³And I appointed as treasurers over the storehouses Shelemiah the priest, Zadok the scribe, and Pedaiah of the Levites, and as their assistant Hanan the son of Zaccur, son of Mattaniah, for they were considered reliable, and their duty was to distribute to their brothers. ¹⁴Remember me, O my God, concerning this, and do not wipe out my good deeds that I have done for the house of my God and for his service.

¹⁵In those days I saw in Judah people treading winepresses on the Sabbath, and bringing in heaps of grain and loading them on donkeys, and also wine, grapes, figs, and all kinds of loads, which they brought into Jerusalem on the

Sabbath day. And I warned them on the day when they sold food. [16]Tyrians also, who lived in the city, brought in fish and all kinds of goods and sold them on the Sabbath to the people of Judah, in Jerusalem itself! [17]Then I confronted the nobles of Judah and said to them, "What is this evil thing that you are doing, profaning the Sabbath day? [18]Did not your fathers act in this way, and did not our God bring all this disaster on us and on this city? Now you are bringing more wrath on Israel by profaning the Sabbath."

[19]As soon as it began to grow dark at the gates of Jerusalem before the Sabbath, I commanded that the doors should be shut and gave orders that they should not be opened until after the Sabbath. And I stationed some of my servants at the gates, that no load might be brought in on the Sabbath day. [20]Then the merchants and sellers of all kinds of wares lodged outside Jerusalem once or twice. [21]But I warned them and said to them, "Why do you lodge outside the wall? If you do so again, I will lay hands on you." From that time on they did not come on the Sabbath. [22]Then I commanded the Levites that they should purify themselves and come and guard the gates, to keep the Sabbath day holy. Remember this also in my favor, O my God, and spare me according to the greatness of your steadfast love.

[23]In those days also I saw the Jews who had married women of Ashdod, Ammon, and Moab. [24]And half of their children spoke the language of Ashdod, and they could not speak the language of Judah, but only the language of each people. [25]And I confronted them and cursed them and beat some of them and pulled out their hair. And I made them take oath in the name of God, saying, "You shall not give your daughters to their sons, or take their daughters for your sons or for yourselves. [26]Did not Solomon king of Israel sin on account of such women? Among the many nations there was no king like him, and he was beloved by his God, and God made him king over all Israel. Nevertheless, foreign women made even him to sin. [27]Shall we then listen to you and do

all this great evil and act treacherously against our God by marrying foreign women?"

²⁸And one of the sons of Jehoiada, the son of Eliashib the high priest, was the son-in-law of Sanballat the Horonite. Therefore I chased him from me. ²⁹Remember them, O my God, because they have desecrated the priesthood and the covenant of the priesthood and the Levites.

³⁰Thus I cleansed them from everything foreign, and I established the duties of the priests and Levites, each in his work; ³¹and I provided for the wood offering at appointed times, and for the firstfruits.

Remember me, O my God, for good.

This Scripture begins on a very mixed note. On one hand, we see the people obeying Scripture by separating themselves from foreigners, an issue we have dealt with previously. At the same time they are doing this act of obedience, Eliashib the priest was doing just the opposite by providing Nehemiah's chief enemy, Tobiah the Ammonite, a room in the temple. This was hypocrisy at a high level and is a hint at the perversity that is to come. Remember that Tobiah always had his supporters among the Jews since he was connected to some powerful members of society through intermarriage.

How was such a thing possible under the watch of Nehemiah? He was always so diligent to keep his enemies marginalized. Well, it happened because he was not there. He had returned to the king. If you recall, in Nehemiah chapter 2, the king asked him how much time he would need, and it is insinuated that an agreement was made for Nehemiah to be gone for a certain length of time, after which he was to return to the king. Apparently, the agreed-upon time was twelve years, and it had expired. During Nehemiah's absence, much corruption occurred in the society.

When Nehemiah was allowed by the king to return to Jerusalem, he found not only this corrupt partnership with Tobiah, but a whole host of other sinful behavior as well. In fact, the Jews had completely gone against each point they had made in their covenant from Nehemiah chapter 10. We see first that the church had been neglected, the very thing they had promised not to do at the end of the covenant. Second, we see the development of corrupt business practices, and third, we see intermarriage to the degree that some of the children no longer even spoke the Hebrew language.

Interestingly, these breakdowns of the covenant are listed in the opposite order in which they are listed in Nehemiah chapter 10. Perhaps that is an oversight, but I believe the text gives us a few clues that might make us think otherwise. Our first clue is that Nehemiah was absent for an undisclosed period of time. We will return to this momentarily, but it appears a leadership vacuum existed in the governor's role. Our second set of clues occurs when Nehemiah returns and condemns various groups of leaders. He rebukes the officials in verse 11, and rebukes the nobles in verse 17.

What do these clues show us? In the church itself, which was supposed to be the spiritual head of the people, the leadership became corrupt, compromising with God's enemies. When the leaders of God's church turn their backs on God, they are incapable of nurturing and guiding the people from a spiritual standpoint, and they have nowhere to go but downhill.

As a result of the church's being corrupt and soft in its adherence to God's commands, business owners also began to incorporate the sinful ideas and behaviors of the world. Without the church to disciple the business owners, they became ignorant of how to be different and how to stand for the Lord in their businesses.

As the business owners lowered the standards of their businesses by adopting the practices of the world, they thought nothing of adopting the same worldly practices within their families by intermarrying with the foreign peoples around them, even to the point where they began to lose their cultural identity. As you can see, the entire society began to unravel due to the lack of godly leadership in the church. There was no beacon left for the people, no city on a hill that could help them grow closer to God.

This is extremely sad, and it is truly amazing coming on the heels of the mountaintop experience of the chapter 12 worship service. Nevertheless, it tells us that without good leadership, people will revert back to their sinful default positions, which are always in stark contrast to God's Word. From this leadership vacuum, we can learn two things. The first one is that you, as the entrepreneur and leader, cannot abdicate your authority in your business until you are absolutely certain you have the right people and systems in place. Nehemiah may have thought everything was okay before he left. He had appointed two apparently good leaders in Nehemiah chapter 7, and perhaps it seemed as though all was well. Perhaps he misjudged their ability to lead under the adverse circumstances that always seemed to bring Tobiah to the forefront. Maybe these men were not strong or experienced enough to push back against the corrupt religious, business, and political leaders. It is also possible they did not have the positional authority as the king's appointed governor.

Whatever the case, it is clear that Nehemiah's strength and authority was needed since he was able to make reforms upon his return. If you are a strong leader, do not underestimate the force and influence you carry. We hear a lot about building consensus as a collaborative leader. That can be very good, but do not let that substitute for strong, firm leadership. People want and need that.

The second lesson we learn, or rather, relearn, is that one of our primary tasks is to develop leaders who can replace us. This is important in your church, in your business, and in your family. Most people do not naturally know how to lead. It is a skill that must be learned. Unfortunately, many of our churches and businesses do not do an adequate job of teaching and training in this area, and as a result, these organizations falter over time. This was ancient Israel's great problem after Joshua. No leader came forward in the likes of Joshua to provide guidance and oversight for the people. As a result, they lost their way until they finally were exiled to Babylon by God.

From a business standpoint, this chapter provides a classic example of why many entrepreneurs are afraid to be away from their businesses for any length of time. We have all heard that nobody cares for your business like you do, and nobody has the same standards as you. How important it is for our own health and sanity that we develop great systems that help ensure our businesses function smoothly, and leaders who are compensated by their adherence to those systems. At the risk of being fatalistic, though, I will point out that these Israelites had systems in place, but they failed for lack of leadership. We just can never remove leadership from the equation, which is why we must not only remain in the picture, but train up strong leaders as well.

A final reflection on this chapter would be incomplete if we did not discuss Nehemiah's prayers. Three times he prays for God to remember him. Was Nehemiah just praying self-centered prayers, or was there something else in mind? I believe he realized what we should all know, and that is his work would be in vain if God did not superintend over it and change the hearts of the people toward Him. As Psalm 127:1 says: "Unless the LORD builds the house, those who build it labor in vain. Unless the Lord watches over the city, the watchman stays awake in vain." God's supernatural and mighty intervention is the only thing that will enable sinners like us to stay faithful to Him, and only by His grace and power can we expect our efforts to lead our people and train additional leaders will have any lasting benefit. Fortunately, God has a long history of faithfulness, and that is what we must rely on. This is just what Abraham and Moses did, as well as all the other heroes of the faith mentioned in Hebrews chapter 11.

So I believe this chapter is not meant to discourage us, but rather to give us a cold, hard dose of reality. We can view it as a warning. Our businesses are not done when we are having a mountaintop experience, when things are going their greatest. There can be great peaks and valleys, as I'm sure you know, and we need to be prepared in all situations. There is no room for complacency. Yes, we can celebrate God's goodness to us, but we always need to be anticipating the challenges ahead, assertively dealing with the problems of today, and faithfully asking for God's blessing on our work.

View From the Trenches

As I have mentioned, finding and training good leadership at Busy Bees has proved to be the most challenging experience of the whole business. We have suffered great hardship and stress as a result of hiring nice people who did not know how to lead. Our family is not infrequently in the position of having to make tough personnel decisions in order to correct problems. It takes our experience, force, and authority to get those things done, just as it took Nehemiah to implement his changes upon his return to Jerusalem. It is true that we have systems in place that tell us what to do in certain situations, such as disciplinary actions, but it is another thing altogether to have a leader in place who will enforce the policies. This sounds like Nehemiah chapter 12, doesn't it?

Having said this, I realize that I am always going to be performing some kind of leadership training, whether it is formal or informal. We have a good and developing leader in place now, and I see her developing the mind-set needed to help us stay true to the mission of Busy Bees.

Despite the turmoil and heartbreak we have frequently had in the leadership position, God has always been faithful. He could have easily let the school spiral toward disaster, but He has upheld us. He has been faithful and blessed us despite our numerous weaknesses. We praise and thank Him for this, and ask Him to carry our work forward profitably and in a way that builds His kingdom.

Chapter 19

Your Response to God's Word

Now those who were scattered went about preaching the word.

Acts 8:4

G od does not give us Scripture simply as a means of telling us good stories. His Word reveals His mind and will to us, and He desires us to respond to and be transformed by it. Since you have taken the time to read this book in its entirety, I assume you are deeply interested in building a business that honors God and seeks to build His kingdom. Now that you have concluded the book, you are faced with what to do next. You can either ignore it or use it as a model to help build your kingdom business. I hope you will choose the latter.

The Scriptures used in this book are not an exhaustive representation of those that can and should be used to build a kingdom business. There are many more to learn and apply. This study of Nehemiah has merely been a way, through the example of one man, to show some of the principles involved in building a kingdom business. I hope you use Nehemiah as a role model when you encounter difficult situations.

More than anything, the story is about a man who followed God's call passionately and faithfully. Without his heartfelt obedience and planning in his days as cupbearer to Artaxerxes back in

Shushan, Jerusalem may never have been rebuilt, and the Jewish culture may never have been restored. But because he did obey and persist, Jerusalem was rebuilt, the culture was restored, and the way was paved for Jesus Christ to be born in Israel and to walk and teach in Jerusalem.

What about you? What is the call He has placed on you? What is the overwhelming burden He has given you to fix for Him? What is the crumbled wall lying in ruins that He wants you to tackle? Does it seem too big and formidable? Do you feel like it would be impossible for you to acquire the time and resources to get it done? Remember, my friend, nothing is impossible with God. If He has placed a burden on your heart, He will surely provide you with the means to get it done.

Nehemiah was not a superstar, but he served a super God and was willing to be His instrument. How are you willing to be His instrument through the business He either has for you or will give you? Are you prepared for the challenges you will face? We have seen the difficulties encountered by Nehemiah, and I have shared some of our own challenges at Busy Bees Christian PreSchool. Are you willing to trust Him to lead you through the rough times?

As we discussed some of the more detailed aspects of Nehemiah, we mentioned the need to be in the people development business. The text has enabled us to see how the building and development of people is of paramount importance in a kingdom business. Are you committed to forming a great team and helping the team members become as good as they can be?

Do you feel like you are well-grounded in God's Word and can let the Scriptures guide your business, even when you are dealing with unpleasant conflict that may even be directed at you person- ally? Is your business currently operating on scriptural principles? What areas do you feel need to be brought further into conformity with God's Word? What needs to be weeded out because it conforms too much to widely accepted, but sinful, principles?

Does your business have good operating, marketing, and recordkeeping systems in place? Are you prepared for the rigors of constantly analyzing processes and procedures in order to become more efficient and profitable?

Do you believe your relationship with your church is what it should be? Do you hold it in high regard, and is giving your time, talent, and finances to it a high priority? Are you committed to helping it grow and prosper?

Is your family being taught God's Word, and are you modeling the gospel to your family members? Are you teaching your family to conform to Christ, as opposed to the world? What are some ways you can help your family grow closer to Christ?

I give you this list of questions not to imply that you must have everything perfectly in order to follow God's call to begin a kingdom business, but rather as a means of examining the different items covered in Nehemiah's template so you can identify where you might have weaknesses. You need to know these weaknesses so you can be prepared for this rigorous battle, which requires stamina, prayer, faith, and ever-increasing skill and attention to detail.

God has given us a road map to kingdom business building here in Nehemiah, and He knows we are weak and imperfect. I urge you to steadfastly ask Him to lead you and your business to be used as a mighty tool to help build His kingdom. I also encourage you to get with and be encouraged and challenged by other kingdom entrepreneurs and business leaders.

I would love to hear your stories as you progress. Please feel free to contact me through our Web site at **nehemiahworldwide.com**.

Thank you for reading this book. May God lead and bless your efforts to build a kingdom business. Let's get to work.